Lost Leadership Conscience

*The End Of Progressivism In Ghanaian
Student Politics*

Kwabena Brako-Powers

For any enquiry, contact: 0242628164

ISBN: 978-9988-1-7695-2

Published by Fremdek Publishing
Tel: 0245817490 / 0243402196
E-mail: fremdekpublishing@yahoo.com

CONTENT

Dedication

To all progressives in the African continent especially my mother, Madam Alice Darkwaa

Acknowledgment

My first acknowledgment goes to the chief Architect of my life and my family – God Almighty – for the breath of life given us to do wonders.

I also acknowledge the contributions of my Parents and Siblings; Mama, Thomas (cash man), Ofori, Joseph (Kwame Joe), Solomon, Agartha, Augustina, Awo Yaa, Comfort, Lydia, and Emelia among others.

In the University of Ghana, Legon, I express my utmost gratitude to all students of the school. I also thank the following persons for their contributions thus far; Gregory Quarshie (Lepton), Clement Amegatse, Eugene Owusu-Gyakari (Lord Lynkyn), Francis Adablah, Julien Mawusi Cobbinah (Ascorbic), Abena Duma Aidoo (Abendoo), Abigail Awuah Konamah (Pretty), Aba Sekyiwa Nyarku, Chris David Neequaye, Jacob Shamatey (Du-Limit), Andy Dziedzom Gagblezu-Alomatu, Badaru Askanda Adam, and Basil Pomeroy.

In the Ministry of Justice and Attorney-General's Department I want to thank the following persons; Mr. Ebenezer Addo (Director PDMM), Mr. Kwesi Owusu Ansah Amadi (PRO), Alex Koomson and Mrs. Yvonne Frimpong etc for reading through the manuscript thoroughly.

Desmond Otchere (DJ) and Isaac Gyamfi (Zakay) have also contributed immensely and I want to thank them for the overwhelming confidence they reposed in me. And Also to Francis Kwamena Ainoo for the colorful designs given the book

Finally, to all those who contributed to the "brand new me" agenda whose name could not be mentioned here. I say a very big heartfelt thank you.

I

AUTHOR'S NOTE

I who write this book am dead. The struggle for the remnants of the continent's student front with special mentioning of the All-Africa Student Union (AASU) is a testament of the decaying student movements in the continent.

This book should not be used as a story book read for fun. The narration in the book must cause revolution to take place not only on our students' front but also in the entire continent like never before. The youths must lead the revolution in their individual nations to collectively fight the enemies of our development as a people.

The enemies of the youths are still with us today. The corruptions by our national leaders, graduate joblessness in the continent, mass poverty out there, poisoned political landscape in the continent, and official oppression of the outspoken and political victimization have proven daunting enemies of the movements.

Our continent will witness mass unemployment especially from the graduate class if the youth fails to protect the bargain of equal work for equal pay from slipping by. This if not well addressed will send over one million (1 million) Africans into poverty. Form Lagos, Accra, Lome and Lusaka to Johannesberg and Djibouti, the youth must rally their strength together in order to save the resources of the continent from official exploitation without equal benefit to the inhabitants of the land.

INTRODUCTION - *Mud Rush for University*

"The great appears great in our eyes only because we Kneel. Let us rise", – Karl Marx

Getting a university education has always been my heart beat not for anything but to enlighten my understanding on the suffering of my people (Africans) and to be better positioned to humbly put the knowledge I would acquire at their disposal for maximal benefit.

We have read books on poor leadership not only in Ghana but in other African countries like Nigeria, Cote d'Ivoire, Benin, Togo, Liberia, Angola and Burkina Faso among others that has provided grounds for coup d'états in the continent. There was one particular book I read on Ghana in which the Writer described Osagyefo Dr. Kwame Nkrumah as a "despot and corrupt" for using Ghana's money to sponsor his unification of Africa Project when there were a lot of nation-building to be done at home (Ghana). On issues of leadership in particular, our continent has had negative reporting in the Western media for its numerous dictators we call "strong men" in Africa.

From the days our forefathers fought for

independence right up till now, the Western media has blacklisted positive efforts of our individual national leadership as a way of holding us captive in order to depend on their handouts for our developments. They have shown strong opposition to a leadership that is in touch with the people; and they have done everything including sponsoring of coup d'états in the continent in order to have their wishes come through.

The overthrow of Osagyefo Dr. Kwame Nkrumah on 24 February, 1966 while he was out of Accra to Hanoi, Democratic Republic of North Vietnam at the invitation of President Ho Chi Minh is a perfect American Central Intelligence Agency (CIA) sponsored coup in a small country with a lot of clout like Ghana. The CIA in particular has the knack for sponsoring local people (infidels) to the point of putting them on their payroll. The CIA declassified documents on the overthrow of Osagyefo Dr. Kwame Nkrumah should be our point of reference.

Reading about and seeing Africans who are mal-nourished; dying of common curable diseases; and mothers passing the night without food in their stomach and that of their children made me creak. I was more determined to pay my dues to alleviating the suffering of the mothers who could not afford three square meals a day and fathers who could not cloth their mal-nourished bodies. I know a solution to the above challenges must be a build-up determination requiring a common effort from everyone in our society. No one should be left behind and education will serve as the springboard on which future generations would stand to end the issues of poor leadership; poverty; hunger; diseases and famine ravaging our continent.

And it was at this point that I was more determined to get a tertiary education.

I went to the University of Ghana, Legon campus, to purchase the admission form myself at the tune of GHC70 from the Registry. I had some help from a Tutorial Assistant of the Sociology Department (a Department I was soon to be affiliated) in the selection of my courses as well as the filling of the admission form."

Due to the disappointment of our admission processes in the country, I bought the admission form also of the Kwame Nkrumah University of Science and Technology (KNUST) in order to stall unforeseen circumstances. After all it is said that, there is safety in numbers. Meanwhile, the support I received from my family especially my Mum was phenomenal. At this stage too, I drew closer to God to seek His favor even as I went about working on my admission processes. I know of friends who also did well in the Senior Secondary School Certificate Examination (SSSCE) yet could not get admission into a tertiary school of their choice.

In the second week into the month of July, 2007, I

received a call that put a smile on my face. The Post Master of the Lartebiokorshie Post Office had actually called to inform me to come for my admission letter of the Kwame Nkrumah University of Science and Technology (KNUST). The smile I wore that day was short lived since the program I had actually wanted to read from the university was not given to me.

Entirely not enthusiastic about the program I was offered at the Kwame Nkrumah University of Science and Technology (KNUST), I told my parents I was going to wait for the admission letter from the University of Ghana, Legon, before I take any decision. Though I received admission into University of Ghana, Legon, I was handed my admission letter some few days to the school's reopening. I was so tensed when I had not received my letter to the point of praying for some intervention from the Great Force of the universe. In the meantime, Reverend Joseph Gormey – the Clerk of our church had told me that I was going to get admission into all the schools I chose.

His prophesy really came through and I had to decide on which school to attend depending on the suitability of the program offered me. In the course of my decision, I started preparation ahead of reopening. I finally settled on University of Ghana, Legon, for my undergraduate program.

Having entered Legon in 2007, I engaged myself

in many extra-curricular activities, most of them being student politics. And I indeed learnt a lot and gained a wealth of experience in student politics and activism.

This book contains some personal experiences from the myriad extracurricular engagements I found myself doing. Not only that; it goes a step forward to share some pragmatic leadership insights that are quintessential to effective and efficient student leadership. Lost Leadership Conscience is replete with very instructive principles and notes that can revolutionize the now seemingly fettered student leadership we have to one which is more endearing and adequately attends to the demands and wants of the larger student body. The book painstakingly considers the hurly burly of our present student leadership but one thing you can be sure of is that, the insights and lessons outlined in this book are provocative and I am sure, without any shred of doubt that, you will find this material very interesting and one which meets the exigencies of our current student leadership.

1

First Days of a Fresher

"As never before we need thinkers, thinkers of good thought, we need doers, doers of good deeds, of what use are your education to thy motherland if you are unable to help in her great hour of need?"

– Osagyefo Dr. Kwame Nkrumah

I remember waking up early one Wednesday to catch up with an available moving car. I got to Legon campus at exactly half past seven o'clock in the morning and met a thronging crowd. At the time, all registrations were done manually, although there was then the influx of technology. Course registration, hall registration and any other registration in the school were all done manually. The queue was indeed long. The manual nature of operations resulted in long queues.

People were murmuring as they stood in the queue. Amidst the murmuring, people were spotted engaging in the ritual handshaking of friends from the Senior High School and some neighbors from

1

home. The whole scene looked reconciling.

I made some friends who were soon to double as my course mates and roommates. Joshua Laryea, Nathaniel and Martin Tawia became the friends I kept all through my four years.

By 4.30 p.m. I was done with my academic registration and headed for Akuafo Hall for my Hall registration. When I got my room number, I left for the house and reported the next day to do my course registrations, in the Political Science, Sociology, Archaeology and History Departments.

With the tiring day, I went to my room and met three other people. The room was to take four people. All four of us fraternized. But at this point, deep down inside my heart, I was worried of leaving home and its comfort to rather entangle myself for four years in academic work.

At Home

In the house, I was drilled to chains of advice from my parents, siblings and family friends who were so caring and wanted me to chart a path of success and achievement.

I purchased everything in pair and found myself consuming the very provision meant for school. I remember my Mum growing wild one afternoon when she found out that, I had gotten addicted to consuming my Milo, Nido and "Shito" products before re-opening. I decided to report to campus on

Sunday evening in order to dodge the flaming eyes of on-lookers.

On Sunday

I got all my things ready and boarded a taxi to campus. In exactly 35 minutes, I'd gotten to campus. I went to my room. Surprisingly, in addition to my roommates, I met some other people who introduced themselves as "perchers" who are "legal-illegal" members of the room too. I never anticipated that but that was the order of the day. "Perchers" are people residing in a room not assigned to them other than the legal room owners. The school did not have adequate facilities to comfortably accommodate all students so we had to cooperate with our "perchers".

My roommates, the "perchers" and I exchanged some pleasantries after which I offloaded my goods into the locker.

At Lectures

I walked into a room with an over eight hundred sea of faces and struggled to get a place to sit. It was a Political Science lecture. I imagined how interesting the class would be, as the lecturer kept on asking the question: "Is Political Science a science?" Apparently, because we were all freshers, nobody could give an appropriate answer.

With a Government and History background

from one of the best schools in the country — Abuakwa State College, Kibi, in the Eastern Region of Ghana, I perceived the course would be relatively easier compared to the other courses that I'd been given. One thing with the university was that one was often than not given courses chosen by the University itself.

After a while, the Lecturer — Mr. Asa-Asante intimated that we needed a course representative. Upon nominations [of which I was part] and elections, I emerged the winner. This electoral victory marked the cradle of my political success in the school.

Arguably, my new position informed my dressing. This time, I needed to look like an executive. But little did I know that the executive kind of dressing was a characteristic of those who aspired for the Junior Common Room (JCR) or Student Representative Council (SRC) positions on campus. [That's derisive, any way] I remember an incident in the Second Semester when the Students' Representative Council's election for the 2007/2008 academic year was on. I was formally dressed in a flying tie and anyone who spotted me asked one question: "Are you running for SRC President?"

I began rebranding myself and tried almost always to be noticeable and singled out in any crowd, however the membership. I soon became popular. My colleagues however began to grow weary of my pre-lecture speeches.

I must admit that in the course of my rebranding, I missed the important step of socializing more with my colleagues. My inability to do that created a yawning gap between me and especially the ladies in my class. They thought I was an introvert.

I remember talking to my mates one day at lectures and in the middle of the speech, someone screamed from the back of the class. I shouted back at whoever that was with the statement that, I was going to give the opportunity to everyone to speak. The class went riot as if I had asked for their kidneys. The reactions of the gentlemen were that of open defiance, yet, I was not moved at all.

Upon hindsight, I realized that my reaction was as a result of a discussion I had had with the Former Junior Common Room (JCR) President of Commonwealth Hall, Peter Otukunor (Vandal Bola) — a colleague student activist. He told me of an incident which happened one day when he was addressing his hall members. In the course of his speech the students began to scream, to which he shouted at them in order to be in charge of the people.

Nonetheless, the truth is that, any leader must be seen in charge of his followers however weak he or she may be. That was the truth I was drumming home to my colleagues. I was however congratulated by friends who thought I had done well.

One of the greatest tragedies of the students' front has been the inability of the current leaders to take charge of their followers and call the shot as expected. It was in the course of my ambition to launch myself hugely on campus and the country that I began the business of writing as a way of spreading what became "THE FIERCE URGENCY OF NOW!"

2

𝔚riting (a 𝔗alent and 𝔥abit)

"Our Lives begin to end the very day we keep silent about the things that matter"
— *Rev. Dr. Martin Luther King Jr.*

Most great world politicians, dictators and philosophers I have read about were avid readers in the course of their lives. Mention could be made of Adolf Hitler, Benito Mussolini, Kwame Nkrumah, Karl Marx, Barrack Obama, Abraham Lincoln, Malcolm X, Dr. Martin Luther King Jr., Fidel Castro, and etcetera.

In his book entitled "Marx before Marxism", David McClellan asserted that, "Radicalism rejected any idea of balances and checks, since it considered the only guarantee of freedom to be participation of all citizens in the government of the country". With this premise, the actions of persons like Dr. Kwame Nkrumah, Fidel Castro and Malcolm X, among others, were orientated towards that end.

In September, 2007, Kwadwo Oppong Nkrumah the presenter of Joy Fm Morning Show interviewed

Professor Maxwell Owusu (a Ghanaian Professor at Michigan University) on the reading habit of Ghanaians.

I must confess that, it was this interview that changed my mind set about reading. According to him, Ghanaians read only three kinds of books inter alia; Christian literature, love books and handouts (to the students). Upon careful examination, I grasped the truth in his assertion.

Armed with this information about the lack of interest in reading among Ghanaians, I set out to become an avid reader. Most established and accomplished writers will advice that the first steps in becoming a writer is to be a good reader of books. If you want to develop a good writing habit try to be simply curious and that means read a lot.

Any writer who does not read gets lost in the vortex of mediocre literature proliferating in the world. Sadly, the Ghanaian literature market is still young after over fifty-three (53) years of independence. Our journalism market is fraught with lack of innovation and creativity even from the major media houses including government owned ones.

Generally, readers can be classified into three groups;

1. Those who believe everything they read.

2. Those who no longer believe anything

3. Those who critically examine what they read and form their judgments accordingly.

Numerically, the first group is by far the strongest composed of the broad masses of the people. The second group is smaller, being partly composed of those who were formerly in the first group and after a series of bitter disappointments, are now prepared to believe nothing of what they see in print. They hate articles. Either they do not read them at all or they become exceptionally annoyed at their contents which they hold to be nothing but congeries of lies and misstatements. The third group is easily the smallest in Ghana, made up of real intellectuals whom natural aptitude and education have taught to think for themselves and who in all things form their own Judgments while at the same time carefully sifting what they read. Writers appreciate this type of readers only with a certain amount of reservation. Which of the readers category do you belong?

I started to put my thoughts on certain ills going on in the school and in the country in the form of an article for readers. I published them on the various halls' notice boards. I wrote my articles first under the name, "The University Lens", and later to the "Lens" in Level 100 second semester.

Getting to the end of the semester, I settled on "Austin Powers" as my pen name for all my articles. I soon inundated campus every Monday with my knifing opinions on issues which became popular on campus.

Some selected copies of my articles shall be included in the Appendix. Some captivating titles included;

1. Separation of Powers in Akuafo; an urgent call (2007)
2. Obaahemaa's SRC and the Sphinx (2008)
3. Legon, the Shadow of a decaying nation (2/03/2009)
4. The Apocalypse (2009)
5. Alfred Tetteh Konu is wrong (the case of a former Registrar of UG who enjoyed free education)
6. The Fierce Urgency of Now! (2009)
7. The Urine of a Goat (2009)
8. Authorities Exposed (2009)
9. Aden? (2009)
10. Electoral Commissioner in trouble (2009)
11. Oja ooo Oja (2010)

One thing I realized in publishing an article on campus was that, articles which featured captivating and controversial titles got a wider readership. Interestingly, everyone with bated breath waited for the Monday edition of my articles.

The widening of my readership came with popularity and other consequences.

Lost Leadership Conscience

Below is one such thought-provoking article I released on 2/03/2009 entitled; Legon the Shadow of a Decaying Nation:

Legon, the Shadow of a Decaying Nation

Not knowing something is not as dangerous and hazardous as not wanting to know.

Fellow Students, I have almost always been an advocate for student leaders who are vibrant, selfless, courageous, fearless, and student leaders who believe that something can be done to change the status quo.

Let me take this opportunity to share some very important thoughts with you as colleagues. I should hope we all agree that the quality of education in this country is on a sharp and unabated decline these days.

This projects a threat to human resource development in Ghana and Africa thereby undermining development ambition of this nation.

It is a result of the above that the 2009 Times Higher Education Rankings was not a surprise at all to me. I was not in the least surprised when it was reported on 18 November, 2005 by the Times Higher Education Rankings which placed the University of Ghana 46th out of 100 universities in Africa and 5794 in the world. Kwame Nkrumah University of Science and Technology (KNUST) ranked 62nd in Africa and 6405 in the world. It was *appalling to realize that University of Cape Coast, University of Education, Winneba and the University for Development Studies could not even make it to the list.*

Fellow students' though the credibility of any cross-country statistical comparison is in doubt, the criteria used by the Times Higher Education Ranking made someone like me give in due to its reality. The criteria included; research output, published articles of staff, teacher/student ratio, political interference in university, and employers ratings of graduates among others

The National Council for Tertiary Education (NCTE) statistics for the 2003/2004 academic year revealed that, in the University of Ghana, the Lecturer/Student ratio should be 1:12 for science and 1:18 for the humanities but in reality it was 1:14 for science and 1:52 in the humanities. For Kwame Nkrumah University of Science and Technology, it should be 1:12 for science, 1:18 for humanities, 1:8 for medicine, and 1:12 for pharmacy. In reality it was 1:29 for science, 1:33 for humanities, and 1:14 for medicine and 1:18 for pharmacy. This trend is similar to the other universities and this is why I said the rankings contain some truth.

It is premised on the above among others that there is a basis for us to admit as a people that quality indeed has eluded us and we must be poised to salvage our existing universities from being blacklisted. This year, the ranking of the University of Ghana is nothing short of five thousand and over. This is part of the reasons why I was conclusive in saying that, "Legon is an epitome of decaying intellectuals

This article soon became the talk of town especially among the student leaders on campus.

I must at this stage say that, I did not begin by writing fluently as some asserted. I started with my first article in the school entitled "Separation of Powers in the hall" (in direct response to the lack of separation of powers in Akuafo Hall, 2007). This maiden article brought me some political friends like Joshua Kyeremanteng who later contested for Presidency in the 2008/2009 SRC election. It is without any doubt that, Joshua Kyeremanteng contributed immensely to some aspect of my "radical" nature.

He recommended I read books like Samuel Okudzeto Ablakwa's "State of Coma" (a book about student struggle on Legon campus and in the country in general), speeches from people like Rev. Dr. Martin Luther King Jr. "I have a Dream" given in August, 1964 and Malcolm X speeches, among others. He also contributed in bringing life into my articles through my catchy bold headings.

Though I had read a lot of books from both liberal and socialist writers, I must acknowledge that, my thoughts and actions were largely shaped by writers and speakers like Malcolm X, Rev. Dr. Martin Luther King Jr., Karl Marx, Elijah Mohammed, Adolf Hitler, Fidel Castro, Ernesto Che Guevara,

John Locke, Thomas Paine, Thomas Hobbes, Rosa Parks and Eva Peron (Argentina). These are rare species with beautiful minds that have overwhelmed the world with their strong opinions till date.

Contrary to popular opinion, I believe with socialist mindsets, we the people of the world will be able to create the needed atmosphere for cordiality, equality, social justice, solidarity, prosperity and brotherliness to prevail instead of the poverty, inequality, injustice, mischief, hunger, and the zero sum game that characterized the world market. I also authored various petitions to the Akuafo Hall management of the University of Ghana, Legon.

My first petition in the school was dated 6 June, 2008. I wrote this with a friend who later became the President of TESCON — Legon (the student wing of the New Patriotic Party). We addressed the petition to the Hall Master and copied the Dean of Students Prof. Banoeng Yakubu, the Hall Tutor, Junior Common Room President and Radio Univers. Our petition sought to bring the attention of the hall officials to refund our share of what is known in Legon as the "Predictive Breakage fee of Gh¢20".

'This policy became operational in the University of Ghana, Legon in the 2007/2008 academic year. To wit a friend, the policy 'Predictive breakage fee of GHC20' is likened to one being arrested and imprisoned for no crime committed and that later on when you commit a crime you would not be punished because you had already suffered the consequences. The policy saw the deduction of GHC20 from all Level 100's as a guarantee in the event they destroy university property. As a result of the petition, we were able to rally more first year students to the Hall Tutors office to demand the refund of our money. This was the first mass action witnessed in the hall after so many years of depriving inmates of their rights. The Hall Tutor Dr. Stephen Ahiawordor was hugely surprised and had to come out to calm the nerves of the students down.'

On 14 September, 2009 I co-petitioned a letter to the Akuafo Hall Master bringing to his notice the incessant increase in the prices of food items in Excel Farmers (a shop in the hall). The Chief Petitioner Bright Appertey had grown impatient with the shop owner of Excel Farmers for increasing especially the price of a loaf of bread that sold for GH¢0.40ps which they were then selling at GH¢0.50ps.

It is sometimes funny to see people who spins injustice shiver at the sight of a mass action and intense public reaction. The shop owner upon receipt of the petition arranged a meeting and apologized profusely that, she had no knowledge of the increase and that her shop attendants had done that without her knowledge. I knew that her innocence was doubtful but in fact we listened as she tried hard to convince us. She however, reduced the price of the bread the next day to GH¢0.40ps. Though we felt a pang of victory, we knew deep down our hearts that the greater struggle was about starting. With this background I decided to settle the internal conflict of Activism in the School.

3

Personal Adventure vs . Societal Demands

"Therefore what the people in our country need most is knowledge if what we want to do is to create conscience".

- Fidel Castro -

The Great Book talks of a kind of conflict between the sinful nature and the spirit. It says, "For the sinful nature desires what is contrary to the spirit and the spirit what is contrary to the sinful nature. They are in conflict with each other, so that you do not do what you want. But if you are led by the spirit you are not under law", (Gal 5: 17-18).

On the contrary, the conflict I am going to talk about is not between the sinful nature and the spirit as addressed by the Great Book but rather, it is a gnawing conflict between personal achievements and societal [and parental] expectations.

Parents place a lot of expectation on their children. And that is a good thing. In Ghana, the expectations of parents have revolved around these lines: that their children go to [good] schools; learn very hard; secure good jobs upon completion; earn huge salary in the work place; and in turn take of care family members. These are the customs and conventions upon which our Ghanaian society is predominantly structured.

Parents do not want to see their children engage in activities replete with risk. This is manifested in the copious advice that one receives when setting out for school.

I received many pieces of such advice from my Mum, siblings and family friends who genuinely wanted my good. I was told to learn hard, desist from bad companies, respect authorities, be prayerful, and desist from arguing with university officials.

Though these pieces of advice are good, strict and religious adherence to it in our Ghanaian society has contributed to the kind of timidity we see today in our children. Let us take the advice that says we should desist from arguing with university officials. This advice has made people timid in our society. Open insistence on ones right and disagreeing with a lecturer are seen as crimes in Ghana punishable by convention.

In 2009, I remember disagreeing with my Developmental Studies Lecturer in Level 200. She condemned and bastardized Socialism and

Communism (topics I had extensively read about). I stood up in class and asserted my point which was at variance with what she made the class to believe. After speaking, I saw the disappointment not only on the face of the Lecturer but also on that of my colleagues who were so much consumed by our societal philosophy. I was later nicknamed, "Karl Marx" by my course mates for my show of courage.

Barack Obama, President of the United States in the course of his 2008 campaign tours said that, "if we aren't willing to pay a price for our values, if we aren't willing to make some sacrifices in order to realize them, then we should ask ourselves whether we truly believe in them at all".

I think the true values of our society have not been unearthed. The cowards we see in our national leaders and also that of our children is disgusting.

Our national leaders are afraid of holding strong opinions on issues of the world; politicians are afraid of talking against their leaders even when they are wrong; and university officials clamp down on students who speak and write against them. Consequently our nation has become a nation full of hypocrites and people pleasers. At best we can be described as a people of pleasers.

Arguably, Ghana, under Dr. Kwame Nkrumah, was a country with a lot of prospects; feared by enemies; love and admired by friends; and hailed for its leadership role in the continent. Can that be said of the Ghana we have today?

We have had a lot of things wrong. Even our educational system has become messy to the extent that products coming from our tertiary schools lack the spark that has informed technological revolutions in the world today. Creativity and innovation have evaporated from our society.

Our nation has enjoyed trivialities for long. We have to build a more solid society for our children based on good values that teach courage, creativity and innovation.

As a result of the "value conflicts" currently taking place in our country, citizens who have had western education could scarcely appreciate and admire our values. They do advocate for a more dynamic one.

Look through the hearts of history books and you will grapple with the fact that, Africans are creative people. We have done a lot in the past. In the days of the great empires of our continent, the Malian Empire, the Songhai Empire, the Ghana Empire and in ancient Egypt, among others, we shared the light of our creativeness with the world.

We've never been timid as is seen today. We may have gone through dark chapters in the past but that should embolden us instead of making cowards of us.

Societal expectations [parental ones] and personal aspirations therefore had a great toll on me when I was deciding to join the business of advocating for the rights of my colleagues students in my second year.

I took myself through some thought-provoking questions:

- Am I ready to suffer for students? Would I suffer victimization which is common on University of Ghana on behalf of my colleagues?

- What would my parents say if they find out that instead of learning (which is the main reason for being in school) I was "fighting" for students rights (which is replete with risk) in the school?

- Should I been sacked from school, how would my parents take this? Could I take their disappointment for getting myself sacked from the school?

These were some of the internal questions constantly racing through my mind. I know some of you out there may be experiencing such conundrums, if not worse crises, in your student life. Taking a decision of this nature is eternal and it demands courage from your end.

The hearts of students across the continent are filled with such extraordinary stories of selfless student leaders like Steve Biko during the apartheid regime of South Africa. He was murdered for standing with his people against racist and apartheid regime of the country he loved so much.

Dr. Kwame Nkrumah at a point in time in his life had to resolve similar internal conflicts before joining in the great effort of emancipating the African people of the "mental slavery" well known to us all.

I must caution that tactfulness, a laser-like focus into the future, humility to the suffering of the people and appreciations of their sordid condition are crucial in this business.

Know that there is no middle road to becoming a hero. There is only one long, tiring, and hazardous road yet very rewarding in the end.

If you have decided to join in this "business" then CONGRATULATIONS on your way to becoming a Student Activist. Tighten your seat belt as you ride in the challenges of student leadership.

4

Acting out Believes
(Daring what others feared)

"Observe that anyone who dies for his country is a fortunate man."

Patriotic words from Tafari Makonnen

Unlike in the past, today's student activists are not the conscience of the students and the university community any longer. They have traded their place on campus with persons who want to enrich their curriculum vita. The current happenings on our tertiary campuses testify to the above.

Activism contrary to popular opinion is a selfless venture entered by people who are convinced of their place in history. When you stand with the people in their time of sorrow they will remember you in their time of joy. Knowledge of the population segment you want to defend is quintessential in the sustenance of the struggle.

In Western countries like the United States, curiosity has been the engine behind some of their much touted success stories in technology. However, disappointingly in Africa, curiosity is seen as the highest form of insubordination. When we teach our young ones the good paying habit of questioning everything they get empowered. In my second year, I became too thirsty to know what constitutes the suffering of students and also to explore new frontiers in activism. I began to associate myself with the "power brokers" (people with influence) on campus.

One thing I learned in the course of my activism was that, when you are convinced of the support of the masses for your cause, the status quo will scarcely accommodate you. I defended the students' purse and rights with the "last drop of my blood" – a line I grew fond of. I never missed the opportunity to read, attend leadership programs to develop myself, praise God and own the problems of my colleagues. It was in the course of attending such student meetings that I came face to face with one of the persistent problems of students on every tertiary campus – Apathy.

Apathy is a word used to describe the state of mind of students when they do not seem to be interested or enthusiastic about anything on campus.

Students do not show interest in leadership meetings or attend programs designed for their good. The "spirit of apathy" as it's called on the

Legon campus pervades all tertiary institutions in Ghana. A friend concluded that the student apathy was a fertile ground for student corruption. If the people of the land do not show interest in the way their purse is used by their elected officials, the coffers is bound to be abused.

I couldn't have helped but to agree more with the view of my friend. Students have held the opinion that when we vote for leaders, we are endorsing them to "abuse" our funds. As a result of this long held misconception, elections of JCR and SRC leaders have witnessed low turnouts. There are times a JCR and SRC elections records as low as 35% and as high as 45% on the Legon campus.

Who should take the decision for us?

In the heat up to the 2007/2008 SRC elections, I was in the campaign team of Joshua Kyeramateng - Osei Tutu, Presidential and Vice Presidential Hopefuls as against seven other aspirants led by Elvis Ampadu (De-Trosky) and Allaha. I got to a room to campaign on behalf of my candidate only to be turned down by inmates who identified themselves as final year students. These ladies told me that they have grown tired of voting for one corrupt SRC President or the other and thus, were not going to vote.

Students' unwillingness to take part in a JCR/SRC grew worse to the extent that first year students also joined the bandwagon of non-voters with the excuse that others will vote. I was so much disturbed by students' attitudes on campus. Corruption in the Ghanaian students' front is in vogue because of the loss of the "sense of accountability" on the part of students. The politician will operate with caution if he or she knows that the people who mandated him are monitoring him.

We must blame ourselves for the confidence and trust deficits on the Ghanaian students' front. Our actions and inactions have contributed to the issue of apathy in our students today. I don't understand leaders who are voted into office due to the mountainous promises made to students only to get there and do otherwise.

The sordid attitude of our student leaders is reflected in our national leaders. Political parties campaign on lofty promises only to come to power to satisfy their whims and caprices. Trust has been lost on us as Ghanaians. The difference between the New Patriotic Party (NPP) and the National Democratic Congress (NDC) is a very thin line, sometimes to the point of blurring. Though they claim differences in ideology they implement the same policies to the chagrin of their faithful party members.

It is unfortunate that leadership on campus comes with a baggage of challenges. There are times victories are won in the struggle; and also, there are times defeats and sanctions are leveled on the loud. As if on purpose, university officials and the student movements don't see eye to eye with each other. The list of student leaders who have suffered victimization in the hands of university officials is endless. This phenomenon of victimizing student leaders is all pervasive. Apparently, it takes place in all the tertiary campuses in the country.

Edwin Appiah, Isaac Kwame Batun, Bernard Oduro Takyi, Joshua Kyeramateng, Lord Hamah, Ernesto Kofi Yeboah and Elvis Ampadu (De-Trosky) are few of the past student leaders who have suffered official victimization in the hands of Legon officials.

Edwin Appiah is reported to have suffered a one year suspension from school for authoring an article dubbed, "The Urine of a Goat" – that was a very controversial piece.

Elvis Ampadu (De-Trosky) and Isaac Kwame Batun (Major) all of Legon Hall had their inner rooms locked up by their Hall Tutor for disagreeing with his decisions in the hall during the Legon Hall Congress meeting. Attempts for them to be granted access to the rooms they have legally paid up for proved futile. The Dean of Students Prof. Banoeng Yakubu was again not in a position to help the students as his office mandated him to do. Elvis Ampadu (De-Trosky) and Isaac Kwame Batun (Major) had to apply for an ex-parte motion and summoned the Hall Tutor in court before these gentlemen were granted access to their rooms. Where in the world is this behavior countenanced?

In 2009, Eric Otchere, Isaac Kwame Batun, Nana Gyebi, Elvis Ampadu, Bernard Oduro Takyi, Edwin Appiah and I were arraigned before the University of Ghana Disciplinary Committee for Junior Members for asking the then Pro-Vice Chancellor, Prof. Kwesi Yankah (a man with an unquestionable reputation) in a petition to come out and explain to students an issue that had to do with our SRC leadership trip to Germany.

In that same year, I also wrote an article in which I was critical of the hall Master of Akuafo Hall for surcharging students for soiling the hall's walls. Within days, I had a call from the Hall Master himself summoning me to his office for a meeting the next day. On that fateful day, the Hall Master sent his messenger to come and remind me of the meeting. I walked into the office of the Hall Master only to meet other Hall officials there already in their seats waiting for me.

I was taken through what looks like a drilling exercise. I was asked why I wrote the article against the hall Master; whether or not I knew "perching" was illegal; and finally, whether or not I knew I had to encourage my colleagues to keep the Hall's walls neat. I was made an "Ambassador of Walls" while others were ambassadors of foreign countries. I was not disturbed by threats of other hall officials that they would cause my rustication in the hall should I prove stubborn. At the end, the Hall Master who is a Reverend Minister, prayed for me to become a "good leader in the school and in the country".

The memory of my colleagues who faced a ban on their graduation in the hands of the Legon school officials for "questioning" the Pro-Vice Chancellor is a story worth delving into too in the next paragraph.

Call it a privilege or not, the Legon SRC leadership gets slots every year at the gathering of past and present African Presidents. The venue of such meetings changes every year.

In 2009, while serving as the Editor of the Students' Representative Council (SRC), I joined a group of the council's General Assembly (GA) members to form a house cleaning campaign team to sanitize the SRC and also to instill the sense of accountability in our leaders.

The campaign members included; Elvis Ampadu, Bernard Oduro Takyi, Isaac Batun, Nana Gyebi, Edwin Appiah, Eric Otchere, and me. As the only second year student in their midst, I was soon made the spokesperson during one of our secret meetings in the Jubilee Hall of the University of Ghana, Legon. The group was christened, "SRC HOUSE CLEANING CAMPAIGN".

Our motivation for the formation of the campaign came from a jewel of information we stumbled upon that alleged that, the Agt. SRC President, Ms. Rebecca Delong, and other council officials were due to travel to Germany for the gathering of past and present African Heads of State. We also had the information that the council was charging $2000 from some students to add them to the delegation.

We treated this information with a doubtful eye. We later took the issues seriously because we wanted to avoid the issue of visa racketeering that nearly broke the back of our SRC in 2004 during the presidency of Piero.

Together with Clement Amegatse (former Intelligence Committee Chairman of the SRC – 2010) we consistently asked the Agt. SRC President whether she had knowledge of the said trip but she denied knowledge of it. The council's Press Secretary, Kwabena Boadi also denied knowledge of the trip.

In the midst of these denials, we addressed a petition to the Pro-Vice Chancellor to get some answers since he's the highest authority when it comes to student affairs. We also released some names of persons due to travel to the said trip. I signed the petition as the Chief Petitioner with supplementary signatories from the other CAMPAIGN team members. The aim of our petition was to ask some "harmless" questions from the Pro-Vice Chancellor, Prof. Kwesi Yankah. Little did we know that the intention of our petition would be misconstrued by the Pro-Vice Chancellor and the then Registrar, Mr. Alfred Tetteh Konu.

While we waited for a response from the university officials, the CAMPAIGN team started with a VOTE OF NO CONFIDENCE in the Agt. SRC President. In a matter of a week, the CAMPAIGN was invited for a meeting at the Pro-Vice Chancellor's office. We never anticipated the kind of meeting we attended with the Registrar acting as the secretary.

We were told the CAMPAIGN had incriminated the Pro-Vice Chancellor and the Agt. SRC President by alleging the distortion of $2000 from students. The CAMPAIGN members were told that, we had no authority to, "call the Pro-Vice Chancellor to come out and explain to students" his involvement in the said trip. At the meeting, I became the object of discussion by the university officials. I received a lot of threats for daring at my level to take such a stand against university officials.

At the end of the meeting, the Pro-Vice Chancellor demanded we apologized but we declined. We were promised of further sanctions as a result of our defiance. Our refusal to apologize to the Pro-Vice Chancellor placed us within the claws of the school's Disciplinary Committee for Junior Members which we were summoned in the months of May, June and July.

Meanwhile, our results were blocked on the university's website. We could no longer track our performances online and whatever documents we requested from the Registry bore the heading, "Results Withheld".

In my entire four years stay on the Legon campus, I have led actions against both colleague student leaders and school officials alike. I have always believed in the cliché that, "charity begins at home", and it is in acting out this believe that in the 2009/2010 academic year, Gregory Quarshie (Lepton), Jacob Shamatey (Du Limit), Akonfem, Bright Appertey (Kaliber), Clement Amegatse and I formed a group that came to be known as, "Friends of Akuafo (FOA)" in the university. We used the platform to hold our leaders be it JCR or SRC accountable to the students.

In 2010, the then President of Akuafo Hall Junior Common Room (JCR), Jeffrey Amoako made some constitutional mistakes by appointing a level 200 student into the position of a Deputy Electoral Commissioner of the JCR. FOA sent a delegation in which I was part to the President's office to advise him to tread cautiously but he never listened. We gave him some days to revoke the appointment of the Deputy Electoral Commissioner since he never met the constitutional requirements. When all attempts to get our President to do the bidding of the constitution failed, FOA visited court actions on him and we prevailed on our team of lawyers to cause the impeachment of the President. Realizing what we might do, the President came to the group pleading for us to take the case out of court.

At the final hearing, the Judge ruled in favor of the constitution that, the said gentleman be relieved of his position immediately and also pleaded with our lawyers to drop the impeachment process with the excuse that, the President was ignorant of the detail in the constitution. The group not satisfied with the ruling of the court petitioned for an emergency Senate meeting (meeting of legislators of the hall) to consider the impeachment of the President Jeffrey Amoako.

At the gathering, it was moved that, the Vice President, Fatimatu Abubakr chaired the meeting but when the floor was opened for discussions and subsequent impeachment of the President she deliberately failed to call any of FOA members till someone moved for the President to be pardoned. The group grew so furious that, I sent the Vice President a message that read, "*As you work hard for your paper CV, be assured that, some of us are keeping oral CV of you.*" Though Jeffrey Amoako escaped impeachment in the hands of Friends of Akuafo (FOA) members, some sense of accountability was brought to bear on JCR members. It's no doubt that, the work of FOA contributed to the kind of political nous that is associated with inmates of Akuafo hall of the University of Ghana, Legon.

The telling of these stories is not intended to point out the wrongs of either university officials or our colleague student leaders to you. Though there have been times student leaders have had a lot of things wrong, we must all endeavor to right the wrong immediately. It is alleged that, Dr. Vladimir Antwi Danso (former Dean of Students) has had to withhold certificates and results of some student leaders for "unwisely" misappropriating student funds in the school. However, I think all of us ought to share part of the blame for the "ugly" leadership our student movements had to grapple with.

Student leaders of today have reneged on their roles as advocates and champions of the masses. They are rather milking the poor people of their little privileges.

When is enough really enough?

We must learn to defend the rights and privileges of students with the understanding that, this is a struggle bequeathed to us by our predecessors. A life for a life; a life for the future were their watch words.

Personally, I would prefer death to a life of oppression and suppression where there is no freedom. Let us keep ourselves free by speaking against pernicious laws.

The truth is that, after all the victimization that we went through in the hands of the Legon officials, we did not whisper a word to any student. We didn't want to dash their confidence in the body we loved so much – SRC.

For the work to continue, we must not always refer to our challenges rather, the victories won for the movements should be used to embolden every tom dick and harry. When you are down as a leader, the confidence of your people also goes down and they go dumb. Let us motivate them by recounting historic and inspiring stories worth savoring to them. Let us teach them that the principles of good leadership revolves around honesty, loyalty, selflessness, determination, hope, perseverance, love, and integrity without which leadership will be thrown to the dogs. We must endeavor to be, above all, the conscience of the people we represent.

5

SRC President of All Persons

*"... we charge you with the responsibility to lead
our peoples and Continent into the new world of the
next century – which must be an African Century
– during which all our people will be freed of the
bitterness born of the marginalization and degradation
of our proud continent of Africa."*

- Nelson Mandela -

The National Union of Ghana Students (NUGS) – a body established in 1965 by the extraordinary works of student leaders of University of Ghana (UG); Kwame Nkrumah University of Science and Technology (KNUST); University of Cape Coast (UCC); and the University of Education, Winneba (UEW) has served as the voice of students ever since.

NUGS is in no doubt a great institution. However, its reputation has been marred by petty squabbles between executives.

Like every challenges there is the starting point to the numerous infightings currently persisting in the mother student front. This infighting has been so severe that, the other blocs under the union like the University Students' Association of Ghana (USAG) and the Trainee Teachers' Association of Ghana (TTAG) among others have been left disillusioned with the possible way out of this doldrums.

The genesis of NUGS problems can be attributed to the days of Haruna Iddrisu when he was the President of the Union in 1997. It actually began after he signed the "suicide pact" with the Rawlings Government infamously called the Akosombo Accord in which students were to share their cost of education with the Government of Ghana.

According to the 1997 Akosombo Accord, the costs of students' education were to be shared in the following percentages;

- Government   70%
- Students or parents   10%
- Institution   10%
- Corporate Ghana   10%

The total of the above should give us one hundred (100%). After the pact was signed between the student leaders and the Government, our leaders went to sleep. The NUGS President, Haruna Iddrisu, and his other executives slept so deeply to the point of failing to notice that the Government and the corporate institutions share of the pact had been heaved on students. The Government's share of 70% and the corporate Ghana's share of 10% had been shifted unto the students or parents.

In 2010 during a stakeholders' forum on education held at the College of Physician and Surgeon under the Ministry of education, there was a general consensus that the Government of Ghana has shifted its responsibility unto students and they were suffocating. Other means of funding education were explored including holding corporate Ghana responsible for the negligence since they were the largest beneficiary of products coming from our tertiary schools.

Another appalling issue is that, a non-negotiated understanding among national executives often than not results in the union having to burden itself with two presidents. In the 2010/2011 and the 2011/2012 academic years for example, NUGS had two persons both addressing themselves as the President of the Union without any sense of shame. No one came close at predicting the occurrence of this "stinking" reputation sinker for the mother students union.

A contributing factor to the above issue is the fact that, the Union has become attracted to the two dominant parties in Ghana – New Patriotic Party (NPP) and the National Democratic Congress (NDC) both wrestling to take control of the mother student union. Sad to note that these two parties see their survival in the nation's political terrain as tied up to the apron string of the student movement and they have sparred nothing in their attempt to divide the union.

The union has also witnessed issues of Government-sponsored impeachments of NUGS Presidents. The years 2005 and 2010 will go down into the annals of the union because of its peculiarity and the wanton impeachments of Samuel Okudzeto Ablakwa (University of Ghana, Legon) and Abotchie Afreyie (University College of Management Studies – UCOMS) respectively.

My passion in NUGS emanates from its founding ideals and documents, which this generation has ignored to the detriment of the Ghanaian students resident both in and outside Ghana. We have traded our place in history with the politician for peanut.

The Legon SRC is the mother of all student councils in the country and has since then served the undisputable role of a caretaker for the National Union of Ghana Students (NUGS) and its leadership. The Council has also played a leading role in shaping the direction of national Government on issues of development. National Governments get praised for their good intentions and at the same time receive a barrage of criticisms and mass action for being insensitive to the plights of poor Ghanaians.

The best magic in the Ghanaian student front is the issue of solidarity. In Legon, the solidarity and collectiveness we enjoy come from the spirit and letter of our supreme SRC constitution. As an objective of the council, the constitution stipulates that the SRC shall be the mouth piece of all Ghanaian students and students of University of Ghana in particular.

It is with this belief that in 1992, students of University of Ghana, Legon, stood with the students of the then University of Science and Technology (now Kwame Nkrumah University of Science and Technology – KNUST) when four students of the latter faced rustication for allegedly publishing obscene image of their hall master. The students of University of Ghana, Legon, understanding the concept that as students we rise or fall together, had to boycott lectures for 2nd and 3rd March, 1992 until those students were re-instated.

In 2008, when the students of CASFORD hall of the University of Cape Coast faced official ban on their hall week celebration and some students isolated for punishment due to what the university officials described as, "their wanton display of disrespect", some activist and leaders of University of Ghana, Legon loaded a bus full of students to Cape Coast to solidarize with our brothers in CASFORD.

My disappointment today has been why the other schools cannot stand with students of the University of Ghana, Legon when some of their people get the wrong deal from the school officials?

Lost Leadership Conscience

It is our mission as leaders to ensure that the bargain of students does not slip out of hand – the bargain that; we are our neighbors' keeper; that we are responsible for them; and that their rights must be respected no matter what. My motivation for offering myself up for the SRC Presidency was to keep this bargain from slipping out of hand.

Politics either goes with money or people. Anyone aspiring for an office must have either of the two. Anything short of the two is disastrous. In other words, you either have to use money to win more people to share your dream or you have to have more following to spread your dream.

Like Saul Alinsky said, the most effective means are whatever will achieve the desired results in every endeavor and that was what I did in my journey to the "Union Building" as some put it.

The vision I had in front of me was moving the Legon people to the compassionate intellectual society.

The Legon campus like the other university campuses of Kwame Nkrumah University of Science and Technology (KNUST), University for Development Studies (UDS), University of Mines and Technology (UMaT), and the University of Cape Coast (UCC) was fraught with reeking pungent smell of injustice dripping out of the lips of the power wielders. University officials and student leaders are themselves perpetuators of injustice and

41

like Rev. Dr. Martin Luther King Jr. said, "threat to justice anywhere is injustice everywhere".

Student leaders refuse other students appointment with the explanation that the latter were in their opponents' team during their election. There were times also when we crush our opponents ruthlessly.

University officials selectively victimize student leaders who are critical of their misguided policies. As a result of that, many fine brains have desisted from student leadership.

There were times some student leaders have accepted offers of promissory from university officials to allow the implementation of bad policies that hampers the enjoyment of students' rights.

I have received a lot of punishment in the course of defending the rights of students and so were some of my colleagues. I have been arraigned before the Disciplinary Committee for Junior Members several times and punished for being outspoken. There was a time too that some armed men had to beat me, Julien Mawusi Cobbinah and Emmanuel Addo for refusing to back down on an intended demonstration dubbed, "Yen Su Biom Demo". This happened on one unfortunate day when the Legon campus was in total darkness and at the same time facing an acute shortage of water. Call it a double dip. In 2010, as a result of these challenges, students had to trek home to wash their clothes thereby sacrificing study hours.

Julien Mawusi Cobbinah (Ascorbic), Emmanuel Addo and I formed a coalition that would advocate for tankers of water for students. We invited the leadership of the SRC to join the coalition in its advocacy. As the Convener, I addressed an invitation letter to the President John Mark Bekui to attend the meeting so that together we could find some solutions to the challenges.

The next day, I received a letter signed by the Press Secretary of the SRC by name Agana rather inviting us over for a meeting two days later. We were so fumed that we had to write another letter this time a very strongly worded one to the President telling him of his, "inconsistencies", "incapabilities" and about the fact that, we would tell students of his "insensitiveness" to their plights. A copy of this letter was sent to the Dean of Student, Prof. Banoeng Yakubu.

We were summoned to the office of the Dean of Students who was so mad that he had to call the Registrar to process us before the school's Disciplinary Committee for Junior Members. His anger was a result of a letter we addressed to his office notifying him of our intended demonstration dubbed, "YEN SU BIOM DEMO". He tried hard to talk us out of our impending demonstration but we never gave in. Before meeting him, Emmanuel Addo and I had toured every lecture room telling students to join the demonstration the next day to the Vice Chancellor's office to present a petition on our plights on campus.

Before then too, some students had gone to chalk in front of every hall the date and time of the demonstration as well as inciting words like, "No water, no lecture", "no light, no lecture", "no water, no work", "join the YEN SU BIOM Demo Now" et cetera. When we refused to back down on the Demonstration, the Dean of Students told me these words before Julien that, "you are stretching your luck, Austin" and went ahead to slap a penalty of GHC200 on each of us for "chalking on the ground" (offense of which we are innocent).

On the day of the demonstration, some armed men went to Emmanuel Addo's hostel (which was located outside campus) to beat him while he was preparing to attend the demonstration. In the morning of the event, students were gathered in their numbers to join the demonstrators only to be told that, their leaders had been badly beaten by some armed men. The people abandoned the demonstration because there was no one to lead them. In the afternoon we circulated some documents to the students, explaining why the demonstration was called off and why they must agitate everywhere.

It was later in the course of my campaign that I understood the meaning behind the Dean's words since he became one of the fiercest opposition to my candidature. With the Vice Chancellor, Prof. Nii Boye Tagoe, and the Pro-Vice Chancellor, all hunting me down from becoming the SRC President, I did my best to defend the mission.

Unlike the story of the famous Ernesto Kofi Yeboah and the ever popular story of Lord Hamah, I felt it was right for me to tell my own story before it suffers some damages in the rumor mill. When I got to Legon, many stories were told to me and my colleagues. Most inspiring of all the stories were the "one man demo" by Ernesto Kofi Yeboah who was spotted branded in a red band while moving from one lecture room to the other inspiring and inciting students never to accept the "stinking" status quo on campus. And also, the "we are many, they are few" mantra of Lord Hamah – the man of the popular people in all decades. These stories like others resonate with the undying love of the people to fight for their rights however the consequences.

Ernesto Kofi Yeboah has weaved his story succinctly to the delight of this generation in his infamous book, "The Student Manifesto" and so has Samuel Okudzeto Ablakwa in his book, the "State of Coma". Lord Hamah must tell his story. The future cannot be kept in the doldrums of the past. Everybody must be told the true story and that can come from the subject himself.

How can we inspire future generations if we fail to share our stories in writing with them?

As a result of the brouhaha from the 2007/2008 SRC Presidential election re-run between Joshua Kyeramateng (Holy War) and Allassan (Allaha) all of Akuafo Hall, a committee was commissioned by the Vice Chancellor Prof. Nii Boye Tagoe to investigate the cause of the alleged vote rigging and to make some recommendations to control future occurrences. Songs were made by some ingenious students to critique the Electoral Commissioner who was popularly called "Breaker" for conducting an election that produced 1957 – 1957 results for all the two candidates. This was tantamount to an independence declaration for Legon. This time around, it was not declared at the Apollo Ground by Dr. Kwame Nkrumah but rather in front of the SRC Union Building and done by the Electoral Commissioner "Breaker" in 2008. Activism on the Legon campus though dying was lively and rewarding.

There was tension on campus during this period. Both candidates never missed the opportunity to declare their innocence to students with the least opportunity they chance on. The Dean of Students then, Prof. Banoeng Yakubu accused Joshua Kyeramateng for rigging the election – when indeed he had no fact to back his allegation. This man went round to remove some ballot papers he alleged to have been rigged from boxes in the Mensah Sarbah Hall and Legon Hall during the hay hours of the election. I was not surprise he contributed

46

immensely to the formation of the committee. As a de facto member of that committee, he inched the committee's recommendation to favor his clandestine agenda in the school.

At the end of their work, the committee made some recommendations which the Vice Chancellor endorsed as a working document. The student leadership was kept in the dark during these periods. It was the absence of an SRC President that Rebecca Delong (General Secretary) was made to act till further notice. The Dean of Students failed to furnish the SRC leadership with a copy of the recommendation under the pretext of its being reconsidered.

Surprise you to know, it was when the university officials had heard that, their long time "enemy" was running for the SRC Presidency that the recommendations by the committee was revisited and applied in order to flash me out of the SRC race. A report that fails to capture students' concerns

The university officials brought a policy to regulate our SRC election and one of them is that every aspirant must attain a Cumulative Grade Point Average (CGPA) of not less than 3.00. Like the university officials, many students predicted vainly that I will be affected. Raymond Acquah, a student journalist of Radio Univers, told me that he thought I would be evicted – but he was wrong. He didn't know history was on my side.

History takes side once in a generation and in ours, it was on my side boldly. Out of the ten aspirants offering themselves for the SRC Presidency, only two aspirants remained. The election became a two horse race between me and one gentleman called Gyasi. In the meantime too, I never left my colleagues who were "booted" out of the election alone. I did what I could to ensure their comeback but it proved futile. When the news of their eviction broke out, I summoned a meeting of all of them inside the School of Agriculture and promised to stand by them every step on the way. Little did I know that upon all the things I did, some of these evicted students vowed to make sure that I never became the SRC President. One of them in particular vowed to use the money in his account to campaign against me.

During this period, congratulations were pouring in from all corners of campus more especially by people who thought the election was mine to win. I also had hints of the intention of the university officials to stop me from becoming the SRC President. They decided to write a petition to the Electoral Commissioner, Osei Fordjour Nana Kwame, also known as Kabu, to prevent me from appearing before the vetting committee.

My lawyer wrote a very brief warning letter to the Dean of Students, Prof. Banoeng Yakubu, who upon receipt of the letter was denying the intention of the school officials to get me out of the race. The

Electoral Commissioner received a copy of the Lawyers letter and like always, he also denied the existence of such intention only to be called to his office two days later to receive a petition from the Dean of Students leveling some unfounded allegations against me as some reasons why I was unfit for the Presidency.

Truthfully, I knew that would come. I was disturbed and so were some of my campaign team members with special mentioning of Eugene Gyakari, Eric Behene and Julien Cobbinah who felt our efforts were being thwarted by the oppressors. I should also thank Raymond Acquah (affectionately called Dr. Ray), one of the few distinguished student journalists on campus, for the role he played in getting the university's petition across to students contrary to the wishes of the Electoral Commissioner. I was also invited to appear on Campus Exclusive with the Electoral Commissioner to delve more into the petition.

At the end of the radio discussion, the Electoral Commissioner asked why I made the petition public and I told him that, I am a public figure and so was the petition – a public document. He fumed as he whisked himself out of my sight. Julien, Eugene and I photocopied about three hundred of the petition and pasted them on every notice board on campus and distributed the rest to the students. This maverick act of ours generated massive tension on campus and during this time, students began to question the validity of the university official's petition.

Meanwhile, the SRC President, John Mark Bekui, showed opposition to my candidacy. He directed the vetting committee to evict me as demanded in the petition since he didn't want to have any problem with the school officials. He made this known during a meeting in the Electoral Commissioner's office after our second vetting when the Vetting Committee was considering what to do with the petition from the university officials.

It is rare to get good people to believe in you in moments like the one I witnessed when everything seems to be opposing you. The then SRC Treasurer, Gregory Quarshie, SRC Secretary, Abena Duma Aidoo and the SRC Intelligence Committee Chairman, Clement Amegatse are rare species who stood by me because for so many years, they felt it was time for real leadership on campus. They did this by convincing the Vetting Committee to dismiss the petition from the university officials – and it was done.

I am eternally grateful to you; Gregory Quarshie, Abena Duma Aidoo and Clement Amegatse for your inspiration and encouragement. When all seemed crumpling, you offered me your shoulders to stand tall. If I am standing today, it is to your memory.

Knowing that, they could not get rid of me, the

Dean of Students with support from the Vice Chancellor, refused to give the Electoral Commissioner the money to conduct the election. Attempts to ensure the release of the money by the Dean of Students proved futile. Later on, the university officials said they would release the funds on condition that I step down – but I never did. If because of one man contesting, an SRC election should be called off, then our university officials should bow their heads in shame. This is shameful.

I might not have become the President of the council but I was optimistic of a better deal ahead of the student movements. I share in the dream of my colleagues that leaders with good conscience would emerge in the student front one day. Like other stories, this story should inspire the student movement to strive to achieve more. This is a victory for us all since the oppressor dreads our presence. And yes they are right to do so.

Let us work feverishly to regain the respect of the student movements. Our journey ought to move forward. The student movements across the continent must win no matter what, being confident that God's providence is with us in this endeavor.

6

African War on Poverty
(a Part to Play)

"We owe it to all the peoples of the sub-continent to ensure that they see in us, not merely good leaders waxing lyrical about development, but as the front commanders in the blast furnaces of labour, productive investments and visible change."

Nelson Mandela

I often tell colleagues that, I know what it is to be in need and what it is to have plenty. I have experienced both situations in the course of my upbringing. What we may not know is that poverty is a phenomenon that does not only strike at the needs of the body; it also attacks the spirit and undermines human dignity too.

Many of our colleagues grew up in poor homes, but they being poor do not mean that they are prisoners of poverty. And we know they face many challenges including deferring their program of studies for a year or two due to non-payment of tuition fees.

In 2009, Radio Univers aired a program in which it was reported that, a little over three hundred (300) students deferred their programs of study in the University of Ghana, Legon, largely as a result of non-payment of tuition fees. It would not be sheer extremity to state that many of the affected students come from homes where parents receive an average monthly income of GHC120 or a little above that. In 2010, the number of students who deferred their programs of study more than doubled to seven hundred (700) in the same university.

There was a story of a female student who was suspected of stealing colleagues' handouts every semester. On one unfortunate day she was apprehended in the act and was nearly lynched by her assailants. She confessed of coming from a home where parents could not afford the "luxury" of buying her handouts so her stock of trade had been to steal friends' handout just to make up for her academic work. What is wrong?

There are communities in this country where students who sit for the Basic Education Certificate Examination (BECE) record zero per cent (0%) preventing them from furthering their studies. Daily Graphic on 8 August, 2009 reported, "Not a single pupil from the Anyinam Kotoku Local Authority Methodist Junior High School (JHS), near Akyem Oda in the Eastern Region, has passed the Basic Education Certificate Examination (BECE) for the past eight years".

The abysmal performance of the students

became so acute that only eight (8) students proceeded to Form three (3) to write their 2010 BECE. The District Chief Executive (DCE) for Birim South, Hon. Baffour Mensah Takyi, growing disgust at the turn of events held a stakeholders' meeting attended by teachers, parents, school prefects, traditional rulers, officials of the Ghana Education Service (GES) to consider the way forward for the school and threatened to shut down the school if teachers, parents and pupils would not collaborate to frog leap the community from its quagmire. What the District Chief Executive did not know was that, many of the pupils helped their parents in the farm after school, leaving little time for studies, if any.

In their report on Nyamebekyere Anyano, a community in the Western Region of Ghana, Teach Africa, a student based non-governmental organization, interviewed thirty (30) pupils in the year 2009. According to the report, 80% of the pupils cited the following reasons for their inability to attend class:

- My parents said they would not give me food to eat if I failed to help them in the farm
- My mother does not have the money to give me a feeding fee so I have to go sell "pure water" in order to raise some money
- My uniform is not in a good shape
- Thank heavens that, the Ghana School Feeding Program (GSFP) which is an initiative of the

Comprehensive African Agriculture Development Program (CAADP) pillar three of the New Partnership for Africa's Development (NEPAD) that talks about "Food Security and Hunger" is addressing some of the issues raised by the pupils of Nyamebekyere above. However, my worry has still not been addressed. In the midst of the explosion of pupils in our schools, their performance is still nothing to write home about.

Table 1: Trends in Number of Beneficiary Pupils (Regional Analysis 2005-2012) with a deliberate omission of the statistics for the 2007/2008 and the 2008/2009 periods

National	No. of Pupils	No. of Pupils	No. of Pupils	No. of Pupils	No. of Pupils
	2005/2006	2006/2007	2009/2010	2010/2011	2011/2012
Ashanti	8,972	119,360	171,181	181,562	199,629
Brong Ahafo	5,701	61,921	104,424	114,964	158,264
Central	7,796	26,705	41,648	44,248	85,400
Eastern	10,161	35,154	49,760	53,803	103,804
Greater/A	14,817	97,407	127,354	130,714	131,149
Northern	3,084	14,588	40,154	50,597	116,666

Upper/W	2,457	5,598	18,930	21,865	54,571
Upper/E	3,886	11,366	28,331	34,082	60,747
Volta	4,531	11,769	28,084	29,685	88,734
Western	3,370	29,630	48,353	52,111	114,962
Total	64,775	413,498	658,219	713,631	1,113,928

Credit: Ghana School Feeding Programme (GSFP)

With a step at a time, we will overcome the obstacle ahead of us and achieve the goals that the African Union and the Economic Community of West African States (ECOWAS) have set for our continent.

One question that is always asked by students and their leaders has been: what is our Government doing to remedy the situation? We have forgotten that Governments cannot be the source of all solutions to developmental maladies of any nation. As students we have neglected our responsibilities as partners of development. In the midst of deferring of programs of study by our colleagues, we have failed to act.

The Student Council on the Legon campus for example, raises over GHC4 million annually and this is said to be bigger than Ghana Government subventions to the school. I must state that this amount is smaller compared to what the Student Councils of both the Kwame Nkrumah University of Science and Technology (KNUST) and the University for Professional Studies (formerly IPS now UPS) get annually. What do we use these monies for?

We enjoy beach parties, splashy hall and SRC week celebrations, and pool parties nothing more. Gone were the days when students used their monies to support their communities for utmost benefit. In the past, students engaged in clean up exercises in communities with poor environmental issues; voluntarily mobilized themselves to these communities and educated the rural folks on certain curable diseases, like Malaria; and also made some charitable donations to Orphanage homes. The story today is significantly different and pathetically, it's worst.

One particular hall in the University of Ghana, Legon, has been dedicated to our hard working farmers for their contribution to the building of the school in the pre-independence era. These farmers kept faith with time and had confidence in the products of this ivory tower. However, the current trend of leadership in our schools is nothing to write home about.

These days, student leaders without shame boast of organizing one of the best hall week celebrations in the school. A former Junior Common Room (JCR)

President of Akuafo Hall in the 2008/2009 academic year boasted of organizing the best hall week celebrations ever in the history of the hall after spending over GHC20, 000. His administration only saw the purchasing of two poly tanks for the hall but was predominantly fraught with huge financial malfeasance.

How do we expect to be taken serious when all we know to do best is to spend huge monies belonging to our colleagues on frivolous celebrations like hall and SRC week celebrations?

As leaders, our objective is to give people more relief from their challenges and equip them with more opportunities. That is what the students of the university community, be it Kwame Nkrumah University of Science and Technology (KNUST), University of Cape Coast (UCC), University for Development Studies or University of Ghana (UG) want. They want educational training; career preparation seminars; voluntary opportunities to the communities they love and above all, a leadership that will make them benefit from their dues. They desire a future full of unlimited opportunities.

A friend told me that his parents sent him to school to be exposed to opportunities, to help save the family from poverty and to be part of a great nation. Incidentally, the dreams of my friend's parents and that of mine can be met should student leaders learn to make judicious use of the capital that is entrusted in their care.

As student leaders, we cannot remain indifferent to the suffering out there. We should not afford the "luxury" of organizing splashy hall week celebrations while our parents and siblings are ill-claded, ill-fed and ill-housed. We have committed one of the greatest wastes in the life of humanity by being indifferent even to our own colleagues and the plights of the society outside of school. We see colleagues defer their programs of study and we do nothing within the remit of our resources to salvage the situation, huh!

The battle on poverty will be spectacular especially in Africa with over five million people within the poverty line. It will demand thousands of small but great efforts that would add up to a vast national effort like the Ghana School Feeding Program (GSFP) and the Livelihood Empowerment Against Poverty (LEAP), among others.

Achievements of the Millennium Development Goals (MDG's) should be our concern as students. Every man, woman and child should be made to breath the fresh air of hope once again in the continental students front. We have been told for far too long that our youths are incapable. Let us lead the way.

Let us administer to the many problems we spot in our country by organizing our resources and strength to remedy them. During my SRC

Presidential campaign in 2010, one of my pivotal policies was to institute a volunteer program for the students. What informed this policy was the findings of an intense research I conducted on programs and activities of past student leaders. To my shock, students of old organized their colleagues for volunteer programs in some selected communities depending on their needs, challenges and environmental concerns.

This we can also do and do to the fullest of our capacity. The challenges that plagued our communities in the past are still with us today. The persistence of those challenges in our communities emphasizes the point that, one generation slept and that is ours. We must awake from our stupor.

Let us once more take up the business of organizing students for volunteer programs in our rural and urban areas that show signs of lack. A curable disease like Malaria is ravaging our people and killing scores of them. We must wage a "holy war" on Malaria in every corner of our society till every life is saved.

As students, it is our most sacred responsibility to help ameliorate situations of poverty in our country through judicious and calculative use of our resources. It also means that we would have to use the money accruing from the dues our student councils levy all students' in a manner that will bring the good in them. We must begin to let these monies impart positively in the lives of our colleagues and Ghanaians in general.

We can set up a needy fund to support those of our colleagues who will have to defer their program of study due to non-payment of fees and this will put us in a better light. Let us know that for every citizen, including the rich, to have peace in Ghana, the poor must be brought along in the prosperity vault of our country and we as students must lead that fight.

As educated Ghanaians, let us reach out to the illiterate in society and navigate them through the muddy waters of poverty. We must invest in their lives and abhor the habit of misappropriating funds belonging to our colleagues.

Above all, the war on poverty can only be won when the conscience of every citizen is aroused. In other words, we will not win the war on poverty till everyone in the continent sees the suffering of neighbors as a call to action. All hands ought to be on deck in this struggle.

As people in leadership positions, we serve as reflectors to others so we have to be cautious of the life we live. Let us begin to behave as men and women whose memories will be enshrined in the hearts of the future generations.

Kwabena speaking to the Congress men and women of Legon Hall of the University of Ghana during their maiden edition of Congress Week Celebration instituted by the Hon. Speaker Boas in 2010

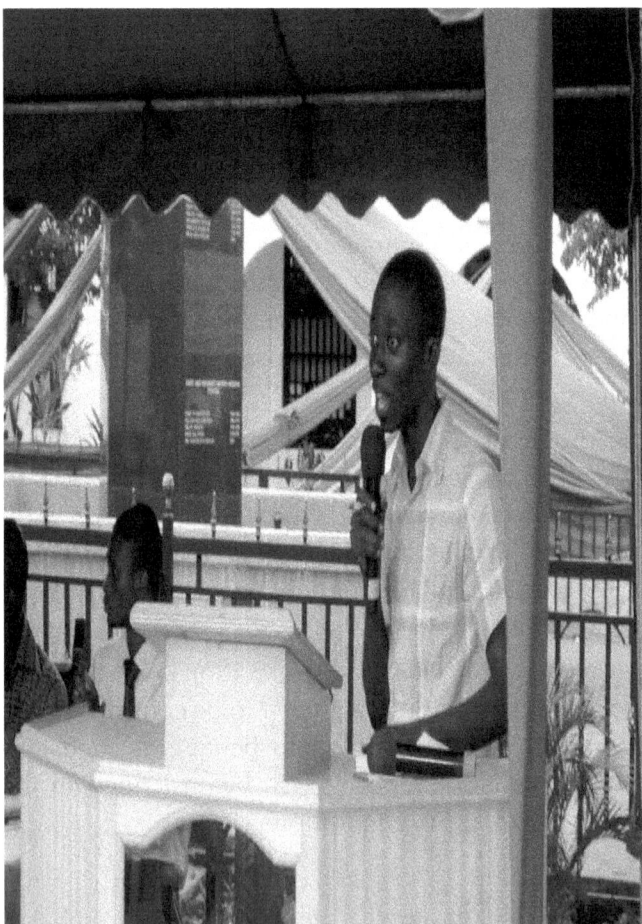

Kwabena at Leadership Summit in 2012 at the India Kofi Annan ICT Center Ridge Office

Kwabena Brako-Powers and his Vice Caleb for the 2010/2011 SRC Election

7

Defects of an African Education

We as students will not obtain our freedom by refusing to work but by refusing to make sacrifices

Since its creation in the era of imperialism, the student movements across the continent have played a vanguard role in the whole business of yanking off oppression of our people. Throughout history, past student leaders like Steve Biko of South Africa among others have been associated with something the student movement can boast about.

Today's challenges facing post-independence African students are not so different from that of the past. The only striking difference will be a matter of degree.

Fact is the circumstances that led to a massive demonstration of Zambian students in 1971 are still with us in this era of democracy. In the past, student demonstrations since the establishment of the

University of Zambia in 1966 had been in support of one Government policy or the other. Protest outside the British High Commission and the French Embassy have been the normal routine of student demonstrations in the past.

However, an incident occurred which led to the closure of University of Zambia and the deportation of two expatriate Lecturers by the regime of the former "strong man" of Zambia Mr. Kenneth Kaunda (Popularly Known as KK by the members of his United National Independence Party).

In July, 1971 students protested outside the French Embassy situated in the middle of Lusaka – the capital of Zambia over the rights granted South Africa (Apartheid Regime) to manufacture Mirage Jet Fighters. The unprepared Police who were also outnumbered by the students did not know how to contain the demonstrators.

An unwarranted riot ensued between the Police and the demonstrators leading to the firing of tear gas shells at students. The Commanding Officer of the task force fired his revolver to fleeing students wounding one in the thigh as accounted.

"By the end of the day, of the thousand or more students who partook in the demonstration, over fifty had been arrested, a number badly beaten up and one lay in hospital with a bullet lodged in his thigh. The police had sustained no casualties", recounted Michael Burawoy in his thesis.

Lost Leadership Conscience

Among all the national leaders who congratulated the students and their leaders for their show of "faith" it was only the President Kenneth Kaunda who did not praise them and described their action as a "show of indignation at the French action…"

In his later statement, the President chided the student leaders and demanded that, in future, issues of foreign policy "should be left in his hands". Enraged by his statement, the student leaders signed an open letter to the President leveling issues of "hypocrisy" and "inconsistency" on the part of the President on matters of South Africa.

With all attempts to make the student leaders apologize for their open letter failed, the President under the voice of Party faithfuls, called for the closure of the University of Zambia and the arrest of some student leaders by Military, the Para-military and riot police at 4 a.m.

So in all this piece of history, what is in it for us as post-independence African students? The issues that the students and their leaders in Zambia had to deal with are still staring boldly at us today. The "inconsistencies" and "hypocrisies" of our university officials and individual national Governments are stinking.

When we attempt to call the bluff of our Governments, they reward our show of confidence and faith with closure of universities as witnessed in

Zambia and Ghana; arrest and torture of student leaders for leading a protest against their "insulting" behaviors that portend gloom to the future of our continent.

There issues of foreign domination still persisting in our individual African nations. The domination of Ivory Coast by France and the imperialistic agenda of Morocco to annex the Arab Democratic Republic of Sahrawi are cases in point.

Our leaders are sleeping while the Europeans, Americans and recently Asia led by Chinese are busily working against us in the international market. Our voice internationally has been shushed. And this has been possible because our national leaders have inferiority complex unmatched in the world. They feel less of a human being when negotiating with Europeans and Americans on issues that hold life and death for their citizens.

The 1976 students' revolt in South Africa popular dubbed "The Soweto Uprising" will perhaps inform us more on the challenges we face in Africa and why as students we have to respond real quick.

As student of the continent, we must learn to have a "foreign policy" agenda for our unions that will be in conformity with the hopes; aspirations; and desires of the poor people. We must address the issue of poverty in our continent by ensuring that our leaders do not trade our resources for peanut or pottage.

"The poverty in which most families lived had implications for many of their children. As a result, the boundaries were not always clear between childhood, adolescence and adulthood. The youth of 'school-going age' spent their days on the streets doing odd jobs and playing, but mostly taking responsibility for their siblings and homes while their parents were at work from early morning until late at night. Many had to raise cash for their families as hawkers (selling fruit, peanuts and other goods on trains and at various railway stations) and others worked full time as providers. Child labourers included 'spanner boys', who helped fix cars and those who sold coal and firewood, as Soweto had no electricity." Recounted in the book published by UNISA Press titled 'The Road to Democracy in South Africa' Volume 2 (1970 – 1980).

We should be mindful that, this bestial modus operandi was going on in the days of the Apartheid regime.

Philip Bonner and Helena Pohlandt-McCormick intimated that, socio-economic issues accounted for the riot. Bonner contends that between 1954 and 1960 a little above 50 000 houses were built in Soweto. However, the rate of this building slowed down in the early 1960s and was completely truncated in 1965.

In addition, after 1960 the government began to restrict and even remove the minimum rights enjoyed by urban Africans, who were told they could enjoy political and civic rights only in 'homelands' like Transkei and Bophuthatswana. The policy shift in 1960 resulted in state revenue and resources being redirected from African urban areas to the homelands. Between 1962 and 1971 no new secondary schools were built in Soweto. The number of African children enrolling at primary schools expanded more rapidly than the resources allocated to the education sector, with some classes comprising more than 100 students. Not surprisingly, teachers were forced to teach double sessions each day.

If the issues of socio-economic nature as alluded to by Bonner watered the ground for the protest, then the enforcement of Afrikaans as the medium of instruction in African schools in 1970 precipitated the "showdown".

"African parents, journalists, school principals, teachers and even homeland leaders opposed the imposition of Afrikaans in African schools. On 3 January 1975, the African Teachers' Association of South Africa (ATASA) submitted a memorandum to the Department of Bantu Education protesting the ruling that from 1975 Afrikaans and English should be used on 50:50 bases — the ruling was actually implemented in 1976 at selected schools."

After the opposition from their parents could not yield the needed results, on May 19 1976, a committee of class representatives presented a "five-point memorandum" protesting against the use of Afrikaans in the school to their Principal. A march to their school board was planned with students from Emthonjeni and Thulasizwe Higher Primary Schools in Orlando, Belle Higher Primary School, Pimville Higher Primary School, Khulangolwazi Higher Primary School, and Senaoane Junior Secondary School.

The striking difference in this protest was that, the schools listed above joined the protest march on separate days in what I have termed a "solidarity march".

In 1985 ANC president-in-exile, Oliver Tambo, intimated that the ANC was ill-prepared when the Soweto uprising began, concluding that:

> *This uprising of 1976-77 was, of course, the historic watershed ...Within a short period of time it propelled into the forefront of our struggle millions of young people ... It brought to our midst comrades many of whom had very little contact with the ANC, if any ... Organisationally, in political and military terms, we were too weak to take advantage of the situation that crystallised from the first events of 16 June 1976. We had very few active units inside the country. We had no military presence to speak of. The communication links between ourselves outside the country and the masses of our people were still too slow and weak to meet such (a challenge) as was posed by the Soweto uprising.*

The casualties in terms of lives lost in the march were overwhelming. Many students lost their lives fighting for dignity and what rightfully belongs to Africans. The next chapter has the names of the students who were sacrificed for us.

Most recently, the All-Africa Students Union (AASU) in 2005 released a report on the manhandling of students in Togo after the 38 years rule of late President Gnassingbe Eyadema, who died on 5 February, 2005. The report which was posted on the internet reads, "The All-Africa Students Union wishes to draw the attention of the African Union and international community to the arrest and detention of students and youth by the military authority in the Republic of Togo".

The report continued that, "In the last 38 years of mis-rule of Mr. Gnassingbe Eyadema, rallies and organized civil protest were taboos in the country. This was an opportunity for young people of the Republic of Togo who have never seen any good governance during their life to come out and express their joy of liberty. Many of them were shot by Togo Gendarme loyal to the ex-dictator, while some of them have, been seriously tortured, raped and remanded in several secret locations in Togo."

The report which was released by the Secretary-General of AASU Mr. Oludare Ogunlala called for "immediate release of all students and youth arrested by the gendarme and also call on the people of Togo to take their destiny into their own hands by organizing a quick democratic referendum to move the country forward".

I am convinced that as students in the continent we are one body inhabiting different individually, and selfishly carved canoe called state. We rise and fall together and our voice will be the bridge on which future generations will climb to the land of prosperity, liberty, peace and freedom so we must act to inspire hope.

The Insight Newspaper of Friday 4 – Sunday, 6 March, 2005 (Vol. 10 NO. 323) carried a report captioned, "Legon SRC Speaks".

According to the Ghanaian paper, Ms. Josephine Adwoa Ashia President of Legon SRC spoke out to Ghanaians and the international community in a press conference held in the year 2005 in which she raised issues affecting University of Ghana students among which includes;

- The annual 20% education increment of fees by Vice-Chancellor, Ghana (VCG) – an association of Vice-Chancellors and Rectors in Ghana.

- 20% and 30% increment in the Accommodation Facility User Fees (AFUF) and the Residential Facility User Fees (RFUF) respectively as announced by VCG

- The unnecessary "dismissal of students for various offences ranging from; academic nonperformance, to minor offences as a punitive measure".

• Inadequacy of the SSNIT student's loan which was GHC120; taking into account "recent hikes in fuel prices and resultant increase in the price of goods and services".

• Security on campus; cases of rape, visa and passport racketeering, confident tricksters, duping of taxi drivers etc.

• Ejection of "Perchers" – the banner headline of Wednesday February 26 2005 edition of the Daily Graphic captioned "Legon to eject all "perchers"'

• The problem of GNATOC; issues of GNATOC members not receiving their study leave entitlements.

• Limited facilities for large numbers of students to an unfriendly lecture hall. "Apart from the rooms not being large enough to accommodate the over thousand students crowding in there for a lecture, the public address system most of the time is not able to reach the student squatting at the back. The blackboards in the lecture halls are not in the best shape to support teaching."

One need not be a Prophet to conclude that, the challenges we face predominantly are internal with fewer coming from the external world. Our national Governments glory and thrive in our silence and have since fashioned out ways of clouding our voices.

We have allowed the "men and women in suit" to put a knife on the things that held us together and now we are failing apart as put more cogently in Chenua Achebe's 'Things Fall Apart'.

Our surprise in the actions of our national leadership is the way they are partly rhetorically committed to ensuring a collective society for all and partly uncommitted in fulfilling their numerous election promises.

As students in Africa, we need an uncluttered access to quality education which will go a long way to addressing the poverty issue in the continent. We desire skills; skills that will enable us to pay our tribute to the development of the continent we love so much.

It is worth emphasizing that, the actions of the past students have earned us the continent we inhabit today however, its myriad problems. So to be able to build on their struggle and lead our individual nations into the "promise" land, we have to be awake from our stupor like never before.

From the above, it is obvious that students in this continent face official opposition and oppression from individual national Government as well as university officials. There are also moments of opposition from our colleagues leading to divisions in the student front. The division in the Nigeria students front leading to two mother unions and the issue of unnecessary student rivalry in the National Union of Ghana Students (NUGS) leading to parallel leadership in 2010/2011; 2011/2012 and the 2012/2013 academic years are cases in point.

Incidents of this nature in themselves lead to loss of confidence in the student leadership by the populace thereby increasing popular support for national Governments.

The 2007 Visitation Panel report on the University of Ghana, Legon indicated that, the views of university staff with regards to students' membership in certain university boards were unsavory. Some officials told the Panel that students could not govern themselves and as a result they "had to be exempted from important boards like the academic board".

We must strive to restore dignity in the students' front across the continent. We will be respected when our actions are devoid of pettiness which has characterized post-independence student movements in Africa. Let us do the right things. They are worth it.

8

Shaping a More Responsive and Responsible leadership

"Warriors are remembered with awe and statesmen
With respect but it is the healers who are remembered
With love"
(Unknown)

Our continent has seen slavery; racism; colonialism; apartheid; military take-overs; famine; drought and neo-colonialism. We have seen them altogether yet we do not look any better than countries like India in Asia that was under colonialism alongside Nigeria, and Ghana among others.

Our leaders are so much consumed in their selfish thoughts so much so that they have failed to appreciate the fact that, the ground upon which we stood some years past has shifted beneath us and we are near to losing the battle in the world comity of nations.

Their lack of direction and consuming inefficiencies in their inability to deliver the public goods cannot be covered by the blame game that is associated with them.

As were of the past, today, we are not judged by our "dark" color but rather by our deeds.

Our primary duties as African students are but not limited to the following;

a) We must guard our individual nations against leaders whose actions and inactions remind us of our past hardships and challenges. This we must be committed to doing in order to safeguard our continent that is enjoying from the harvest of democracy.

b) We must give clear policy guidelines to our national governments by insuring that, quality education and health care are made accessible not only to the rich but also the poor and the impoverished. In 2011 as the Press and Information Secretary of the National Union of Ghana Students (NUGS), I released a statement in which I stated that, achieving the 2015 United Nations Millennium Development Goal (UNMDG) on universal primary education cannot yield the needed developmental impact if it is not tied to a guaranteed Junior and Senior High education. Our national leadership must have a different orientation towards education and this must be for the better. We must change our educational policy from quantity to quality and it is only by insisting in quality that we will be able to fight mass poverty together as a people.

c) Related to the above is the fact that, we must insist that our individual national educational curricula are in consonance with the current world market demands. In Ghana, our curriculum is taking a roller-coaster ride and it is now gathering steam. We are taught courses that make little or no impact in the lives of the graduates leading to what is termed, "graduate joblessness". The system needs to be overhauled for a massive revision to be implemented. Our leaders must know that, as students, we desire to be taught programs that would make us creative and innovative.

d) We must fight poverty and mass illiteracy together with our government and civil societies leading the way. I will not have to recount time and again when students unnecessarily spend their colleagues dues on frivolous things without thinking of how to improve the lives of their colleagues as leaders of the future Africa. Our people would stand with us if we kept faith with them. If we stand with them and share our knowledge, expertise and wealth with the good people of this continent will once again have faith in students and respect our decisions. We have to administer to their needs as inheritors of a continent replete with sacrifices.

e) Finally, we must desist from opposing the policies of our national Governments and university officials without providing an alternative. The days of repeatedly opposing national Governments policies without providing a workable alternative is having a kill on us. Therefore, to experience growth as students we have to provide alternatives to defunct Government policies and sell our views to the people since they are at the receiving end of any policies either good or bad. To be able to do this successfully, we must do thorough research, consult appropriate authorities and verify findings before communicating to the larger world around us.

In the discharge of our responsibilities, we must almost always remember that some generations in the past laid their lives for us to be able to see this day and it is incumbent upon us to follow in their step.

A deceased student like Mekki Abbas – a former student of University of Ghana, Legon who was shot dead during a student protest on the Legon campus [as recounted by Samuel Okudzeto Ablakwa in his book "The State of Coma"] is worth remembering. The roundabout at the university's main entrance has been named after but this is not enough, and we must spread the gospel of past sacrifices and tell the current students that an inheritance of sacrifice is our portion and that we must rise to the occasion.

Lost Leadership Conscience

Also to the memory of the students who led the 1976 youth uprising in South Africa that led to the death of scores of their people.

Name	Place of death	Age	Date	Cause of death
Adams, Sandra Joyce	Kew Town	15	16.9.76	Shot in front of head (ricochet) on 3rd floor balcony
Adriaanse, Noel John	Hanover Park	13	2.9.76	Shot through left side of head
Africa, Pieter	Montagu	24	11.9.76	White Supply. Details of death under investigation
Albern, Bazil	Elsie's River	16	9.9.76	Shot to side of abdomen
Allie, Abduraghman	Ravensmead		7.9.76	Shot in chest from front

Appolis, Christopher	Menenberg	16	10.9.76	Shot in head from front, Jordaan Road
August, Victor L.	Gugulethu		31.12.76	Reported missing during December disturbances
Bakubaku, Golden	Nyanga		26.12.76	Killed by migrant workers
Balnardo, Gary Sandy	Grassy Park	19	16.9.76	Shot through buttock and chest from front, at Head Road.
Barnes, Isaac	Bonteheuwel	16	25.8.76	Shot in chest from front

Lost Leadership Conscience

Barnes, Sydney	Guguleth u	32	26.8.76	Beaten to death by group of migrant workers
Barron, James	Soweto		26.12.76	Shot through the head
Bezuiden hout, Isaac	Mosselba y		14.9.76	Buried
Bota, Michael	Nyanga East		26.12.76	Shot dead
Botha, William	Nyanga		26.12.76	Killed by migrant workers
Botha, Neville, J.G.	Retreat	20	8.9.76	Shot in stomach from front

Buba, Lawrence	Philippi	14	9.9.76	Shot in chest from front
Buthelezi, Leonard	Soweto	39	4.8.76	Gunshot wounds to the head and body
Buthelezi, Joyce		16	26.12.76	Shotgun wounds to chest and head when police fired on students at Sekano-Ntoane High School
Carolissen, Gasant	Hanover Park	21	2.9.76	Shot in chest from front

I don't know how you feel but personally I believe that, like Nelson Mandela (fmr. President of South Africa) there is no easy way to freedom and this has perfectly been shown in our part of the world. Our past leaders fought against imperialism in its rawest form and this battle led to the independence declaration across the continent.

Our generation must not end the fight. We must carry the battle to the door step of the imperialist. Our plummeted dignity and image must be regained by this generation.

An inheritance of sacrifice is our portion and a people of sacrifice are who we are.

9

Dilemma of a Graduate

"Countrymen, the task ahead is great indeed, and heavy is the responsibility; and yet it is a noble and glorious challenge – a challenge which calls for the courage to dream, the courage to believe, the courage to dare, the courage to do, the courage to envision, the courage to fight, the courage to work, the courage to achieve – to achieve the highest excellences and the fullest greatness of man. Dare we ask for more in life?"

-Dr. Kwame Nkrumah

In Ghana, like in any other African country, students take to tough thinking when they are about completing school especially the tertiary schools. You may wonder what they are thinking about. Some common lines of their thought have revolved around unemployment and the poverty out there. This has become possible as a result of pathetic stories coming from colleagues around us who are trying to fend off issues of unemployment and hunger.

In Ghana, there is one common trait that has run unbroken. That is our inability in putting the resources at hand to their fullest use and for the betterment of lives in our country. The capacities of our resources have not been put to work. Our schools, rural and urban areas, the streets of our cities and villages and the edges of our society show it.

I must confess that it was in my final year that I began to think about the work I would do upon completion. It is worth emphasizing that, the lack of creativity in our educational curricula can largely be blamed for the rise in unemployment in the continent. Our educational system is structured on the rot system. In Ghana, we call it the "chew, pour, pass, and forget", system. I wrote a lot of letters to Managing Directors and Managers of companies in preparation for my transition.

[Call it normal] Every other yet-to-be graduate may perhaps be going through this difficulty we call normal. However, I see this to be abnormal. Ghana produces over thirty thousand (30, 000) graduates yearly and only ten per cent of the graduates out of the rest get employment. Burdened too by the freezing employment in the Public Sector by the National Democratic Congress led Government of the Late President Prof. John Evans Fiifi Attah-Mills in 2010 as a result of an IMF loan conditionality, graduates have to see the Private firms as the last hope to get employment.

That means that, the remaining ninety per cent would have to search real deep for non-existing jobs.

The lack of creativity on the part of one means hunger for family members. If the knowledge acquired in our schools cannot be utilized for the betterment of the country as a result of the lack of enabling environment then we must ask ourselves where we are heading as a nation.

I don't know how our leaders feel when they see the youth running to and fro in search of jobs to do. Though I am for hard work, these graduates search for what is termed "non-existing" jobs. We must inform our leaders that, they cannot be partly committed in their ranting of creating employment and partly uncommitted in fulfilling their promises.

I have met colleagues in this country, and other countries in Africa. One thing was clear to me. The students in Ghana, Nigeria, Liberia, Tunisia, Morocco, Zambia and Zimbabwe have same hopes and harbor the same dilemma – not only did they need education, they also needed an improvement in their lives and their families. They will grant justice to others should they be given justice and this battle is lost on our leaders.

This is the real voice of the over 30, 000 graduates Ghana produces every year. And it is one of the greatest duties of our national leadership – to show by actions that they really believe and understand our sufferings.

Sad to know that, though our national leadership pledges to be committed to this ideal creation of employments, they have been greatly uncommitted in making these pledges materialize.

In the midst of all the challenges narrated above, it is important to ask; to what end is our educational system directed towards?

In 2005, one hundred (100) first class graduates from the University of Ghana, Legon were declared, "unfit" for the corporate world by a major multinational corporation in Ghana. Also, the Vice-Chancellor of the University of Ghana, Legon Prof. Ernest Aryeetey in 2011 said in a radio interview that graduates produced in the tertiary institutions are not good enough for the job market. My problem with Prof. Ernest Aryeetey is that, as the Vice-Chancellor of University of Ghana, Legon what has he done to ensure that the lecturers in the school stop dictating 2001 notes to students of 2013? It is happening.

While the issue of unemployment is looming before us, our national leaders go about causing reforms in the educational system for the worst. The issue of the duration for the Senior High School (SHS) is one particular case that has deepened our belief that, our politicians operate on the same tangent and use the lives of the students for experiment.

Both the ruling National Democratic Congress (NDC) and the largest opposition the New Patriotic Party (NPP) have all demonstrated to us that their interest count more than that of the people.

I believe leaving our destiny in the hands of fellow man is suicidal and it is based on that I would want to advice would-be-graduates to take their destiny into their hands. They should strive to create employment opportunities to empower the poor in the country.

If all of us want to struggle for the few available employment opportunities out there, we would be doing a great disservice to our motherland. If outside initiatives like Facebook, Google, Twitter and Skype can be the greatest revolutions in the history of mankind then we as graduates in a continent replete with rich natural resources have to step up our game and win the race ahead of us.

Let us form what I call, "master minds" within our ranks. Form partnerships with colleagues from other discipline. Come out with business ideas by taking into perspective current trend of the individual national market and pull your resources together. In Economics they call it "demand and supply". Knowing the market trend helps you to understand the demands of the people in terms of products or services that are, "hot cake". At this level, creativity and innovation are important. Creativity and innovation have been the success story behind the Facebook's and the Google's in the world today.

Already, in our continent there are scores of

creative people who have come up with brilliant ideas and getting international recognition for that, however, the problem has always been the reachability of those services or products made by these beautiful minds of our continent.

It's important not to limit our partnerships locally. We must equally strive to form partnerships with persons or institutions outside of our country. Though we cannot entirely wipe-out poverty and unemployment in our continent, an effort like this leading to the creation of employment for the growing unemployed youths in our country will complement the work of our national Governments.

Contrary to what I had planned when I first entered into the University of Ghana, Legon – not to work for anyone but rather for myself- I seem to be losing it before my own eyes. The dream can be lost for a moment but not permanently. It will be accomplished and that's why I believe yours too can be achieved with the appropriate steps in life.

Let's not underestimate your influence when history beckons you on. We can and we will make it..

10

Casting a Solid Generational Future

"Popular support is the first element which is necessary for the creation of authority",

- Hitler

Ever wondered how the independence of our individual nations were achieved? Have you come across persons like Osagyefo Dr. Kwame Nkrumah (Ghana), Nnamdi Azikiwe (Nigeria), Julius Nyerere (Tanzania), Patrice Lumumba (Zaire), Jomo Kenyatta (Kenya) and Abdul Nasser (Egypt)? These persons of blessed memory contributed to the independence movements in their respective countries and beyond. They embraced the odds for our forward march however their deficiencies.

Here in Ghana, Dr. Kwame Nkrumah is remembered for his contribution to the founding of modern Ghana yet he is not well celebrated as is done elsewhere in Nigeria, Ethiopia, Guinea Bissau, et cetera.

Among Nkrumah's many state corporations he

established in Ghana included but not limited to the Akosombo Dam, the tire and shoe factories, the Tema dock, and Ghana Telecom etc.

> *"Ghana is a small but very dynamic independent African state. We are trying to reconstruct our economy and to build a new, free, and equal society. To do this, we must attain control of our own economy and political destinies. Only thus can we create higher living standards for our people and free them from the legacies and hazards of a colonial past and from the encroachments of neo-colonialism".*

This was contained in a speech Kwame Nkrumah delivered on the occasion of the inauguration of the Volta Power on January 22, 1966. This was a man who envisioned a small country that commands total control of its economy. Dr. Nkrumah did not wait for the vision to come thundering down to him, he worked towards it and this saw him building the Akosombo Dam to power the enterprises of this small but powerful nation.

The Akosombo Dam today generates electricity to almost the whole country. When the machines at the dam break down, the story in our country becomes distasteful. The generation after Dr. Kwame Nkrumah sought to enjoy the glories of the past without building upon them for our shared future and this should have taken the trend of building over five dams up till now to lighten every home. Today, as of the past, there are many people who sleep in the dark while their children have the luxury of learning under street lights.

The leadership of the post-independence Ghana sold many of Nkrumah's state corporations on the altar of Structural Adjustment Program (SAP) led by Flt. Lieut. J. J. Rawlings and Private Sector as the engine of growth led by John Agyekum Kuffuor of the New Patriotic Party (2001 - 2008). When the Kuffuor Government announced the intention of selling the Ghana Telecom - a company he came to meet, I joined a group called Committee for Joint Action (CJA) led by Kwesi Pratt Jnr., the Managing Editor of the Insight Newspaper, together with the then Presidential candidate of the National Democratic Congress and late President of the Republic of Ghana Prof. John Evans Mills, Dr. Omane Boamah, Samuel Okudzeto Ablakwa, Jude Tagoe and Eric Otchere (a colleague on campus) among others to picket our men and women of Parliament to stop the deal from going through but as always, the deal was passed.

It was later on that one of the anti-corruption crusaders in Parliament, Hon. P. C Appiah Ofori, leaked information about the sale of the local telecommunication company to the British telecommunication giant Vodafone plc. According to him, Members of Parliament received the sum of $5000 each from the Kuffuor-led-Government before endorsing the sale of Ghana Telecom to

Vodafone plc.

Like our national leaders, many students have shed their blood, sweat, tears and some sacrificed their life for us. We owe our lives to a generation of sacrifice that has made us who we are today. Let us remember that it took some students of old to cook what is the biggest and best organized student body in the history of Ghana – the National Union of Ghana Students (NUGS) founded in 1965.

NUGS is credited with the creation of the National Service Scheme since it was the union that advocated for its establishment. Believe me, no sacrifice can be considered too great when it is a question of carrying through the purpose of the student movement. It is lamentable to see student leaders of today, conducting themselves in ways that dash the confidence of the Ghanaian people in students. By their actions, the student movements across the country have been halted and the rights of students are constantly being trampled upon by those who were supposed to know.

We must carry on the legacy of advocating for free, quality and easy access to education for all the children in the country. Our Students Representative Councils (SRCs) must prevail on our Governments and heads of our institutions to do the best by creating a congenial environment for us to excel academically.

The educational system prevailing in our

country today can be reformed when we debate our national Governments on the best possible way forward. We must call for reforms in our curricula so that it will be in sync with the dictates of the labor market locally and internationally.

To lead with conscience, our stock of trade must be to leave a worthwhile legacy for future generations. That means that, whatever we do today must count for tomorrow. We have to live today with the people of tomorrow in mind. We don't have to follow the footsteps of our national leaders who look forward to temporary rewards from the pay masters luring them to sell our assets in the name of International Monetary Fund (IMF) loan or World Bank loan. Had Dr. Nkrumah, Dr. J. B Danquah, Paa Grant, and Ako Adjei, among others of the pre-independence era been short-sighted, our nation would not have had the grounded foundation of a modern nation we enjoy today.

There is a call on your life to leave a legacy that will inspire future generations. How you live this life of yours would be best answered by you. We have to fearlessly lead our generations and the generations yet unborn into the next century. We either out-learn the world in this endeavor or we are out-witted in the struggle for economic leadership in the world.

Think of being a visionary now!

Man, think!

Epilogue

In the world

Students passwords have been: finish school; get employment and live a good life. The question is: is this real?

When I was on campus, I though all was glossy and that when I finish school, I would get a good paying job to do and raise more money for my family. Though this was my dream, surprise you to know that, this is the dream of hundreds of thousand Ghanaian students out there.

Without grudge, our parents seem to be in love with the notion that just by educating their children; their family income would magically swell. However, they cannot be far from the truth.

Unemployment is engulfing our country and this has created the situation of "who knows you and whom you know" especially when it comes to employment. Fairness based on academic achievement does no longer determine ones employment.

The situation has rotten to the extent that, National Service placement has been characterized by corruption on the part of officials of the National Service Secretariat (NSS) each year. Instead of performing this voluntary service to the country we love, money is used to influence ones area of posting. What happen is that, those who pay get placement to the urban areas thereby defeating the founding ideals of the scheme (NSS) – that students should give back what they have learned to their communities.

Gradually, rule of men is taking control of our country that has been designed to be ruled by law.

Politics has become a booming career for the young men and women in Ghana specifically. Our national leaders have demonstrated that, the easiest and fastest way of getting rich is to jump into Politics as a young person and one will not see hunger so long as your party continues to stay in power.

This is wrong. The creativity and innovation of our young men and women have been sacrificed in favor of insult of the elderly in the political terrain. Now, the weight of ones purse is determined by how consistent and effective one insults his/her opponents.

It is noteworthy that, we reflect our national leaders in the way we govern in our schools.

As young people, we need to lead a crusade to sanitize our national politics as is done elsewhere in Tunisia, Yemen, Egypt and the United States of America.

The "People's Revolution" that took place in Tunisia and Egypt in 2011 was led by the young men and women who have grown tired of the pettiness and repressive behavior of their national Governments. The elderly joined the revolution because the youth showed their willingness to sacrifice their lives for the future match of their country.

However imperfect the revolution was, the young men and women were able to topple an incorrigible Government.

Here at the end of the volume, let me bring to memory the adherents and champions of our ordeals, the heroes who in the consciousness of what they were doing sacrificed their comfort for us all. We must never fail to recall those names in order to encourage the weak among us when duty calls.

To all the men who devoted their student life to the reawakening of our people through their writings and their ordeals, I want to say we are eternally grateful.

I wish you and others well even as you gloriously shine in the world. Let us add to our faith, hope and to hope, perseverance and to perseverance, good-conscience and to good-conscience, leadership conscience for a successful experience.

Aluta Continua

Victoria Ascerta

Let the struggle continue

Victory is assured

Appendix

1 Letter from the Electoral Commission disqualifying Powers from the SRC Presidential race

STUDENTS' REPRESENTATIVE COUNCIL
University of Ghana, Legon

Office Location: Union Building
Bankers: Standard Chartered Bank, Legon Branch

E-mail: legonsrc.ug.edu.gh
Website: www.ugsrc.com

28/03/2010

THE ELECTORAL COMMISSION/VETTING COMMITTEE OF THE SRC

Mr. Augustin Brako
10241324

Dear Sir,

PETITION FROM THE UNIVERSITY

The Electoral Commission received a petition dated 26th of March, 2010 from the office of the Dean of Students, University of Ghana alleging you are not qualified to contest the SRC Elections 2010.

According to the Dean of Students, you have disciplinary issues to settle with the University. The following were alleged against you and I hereby quote them seriatim;

1. "Mr. Augustin Brako is facing the University of Ghana Disciplinary Committee for being a signatory to a petition on 15th April, 2009 to the Pro-Vice Chancellor titled "SRC Presidential Trip to Germany" in which he made an allegation of extortion against the then Acting SRC President, Miss Rebecca Delong and also demanded that the Pro-Vice Chancellor "Officially clarify his role in the said arrangement to the entire student body".

2. Mr. Augustin Brako refused to comply with University sanction for writing on pavements and unauthorized places in the University notifying students on unauthorized procession on Wednesday, 28th October, 2009 on an alleged acute water crisis on the University campus.

3. Mr. Augustine Brako contravened University regulations by engaging a law firm to challenge a disciplinary measure/sanction applied to him for breaching regulations governing student activities on campus"

The Vetting Committee hereby requests of you to meet the appropriate offices and/or take the necessary steps to have these issues resolved before vetting on Tuesday, March 30 otherwise the Vetting Committee would be compelled to disqualify you from contesting the SRC Elections 2010. Be advised and act accordingly.

Thank you.

Yours faithfully,

Osei Fordjour Nana Kwame

Appendix

2 Letter from the University summoning Powers to appear before the Disciplinary Committee

UNIVERSITY OF GHANA
LEGON, ACCRA

CABLES - UNIVERSITY, LEGON
TELEPHONE: 233-21-500180
E-MAIL: agric@ug.edu.gh
FAX: 233-21-500180

P. O. BOX 68
LEGON.

OUR REF:
YOUR REF:

COLLEGE OF AGRICULTURE
& CONSUMER SCIENCES
(Office of the Registrar)

13th May, 2010

Mr. Augustine Brako
P. O. Box DC 878
Dansoman-Accra

Dear Mr. Brako,

<u>SUMMONS TO APPEAR BEFORE DISCIPLINARY COMMITTEE OF THE UNIVERSITY</u>

I write to remind you that at the last meeting of the Disciplinary Committee for Junior Members held on Wednesday 12th May, 2010, you were requested to submit to the undersigned a personal written response to the charges made against you by close of work on Wednesday 19th May, 2010.

Thank you.

Yours Sincerely,

(E. Baidoo)
SECRETARY

Cc   Mr. Y. Benneh   -   Chairman

100

References:

The Insight, Vol. 10 NO. 323 Friday 4 – Sunday, 6 March, 2005 Legon SRC Speaks

The World, 24 May 1976/16 000 Pupils Keep up Strike'; *The World,* 25 May 1976, 'New School Joins Strike'; *The World,* 1 May 1976,'Seventh School Joins the Strike'; *The World,* 21 May 1976,The School Boards are Toothless'; Cillie Commission Report

Oliver Tambo, 'Black Consciousness and the Soweto Uprising', in A. Tambo (ed.), *Preparing for Power: Oliver Tambo Speaks* (London: Heinemann, 1987).

The World, 18 June 1976,'Botha Defends Language Rule'.

Bonner, P. L. "The Soweto Uprising of June 1976: A Turning Points Event." *Turning Points in History: People Places and Apartheid*

.http://www.sahistory.org.za/pages/governence-projects/june16/extract-soweto-uprising.html

Brooks, Alan, and Jeremy Brickhill. *Whirlwind before the Storm: The Origins and Development of the Uprising in Soweto and the Rest of South Africa from June to December 1976.* London: International Defence and Aid Fund for Southern Africa, 1980

Hirson, Baruch. *Year of Fire, Year of Ash : The Soweto Revolt, Roots of a Revolution?* London: Zed Press, 1979.

Hlongwane, Khangela Ali, Sifiso Ndlovu and Mothobi Mutloatse. *Soweto '76: Reflections on the Liberation Struggles.* Houghton [South Africa]: Mutloatse Arts

Heritage Trust, 2006

.Karis, Thomas, and Gwendolen Margaret Carter. *From Protest to Challenge; A Documentary History of African Politics in South Africa, 1882-1964*. Stanford, CA: Hoover Institution Press, 1972

Ndlovu, Sifiso Mxolisi. "The Soweto Uprisings: Counter-Memories of June 1976." *Ravan Local History Series*. Ed. Monica Seeber and Luli Callinicos. Randberg: Ravan Press, 1998.

R. Flacks, 'The Liberated Genera-tion: An Exploration of the Roots of Student Protest', i. Soc. Issues, vol 23, no. 3 (I967)

J. Ben-David and R. Gollins, 'A Comparative Study of Academic Free-dom and Student Politics' in S. M. Lipset (ed.), Student Politics, Londona nd New York, Basic Books, I967.

S. M. Lipset and P. G. Altbach, 'Student Politics and Higher Education in the United States' in S. M. Lipset (ed.), Student Politics,L ondon and New York, Basic Books, I967, p. 242.

Michael Burawoy B.A. M.A. Student, Department of Sociology, University of Chicago

www.ingramcontent.com/pod-product-compliance
Lightning Source LLC
Chambersburg PA
CBHW070521030426
42337CB00016B/2050